Learning activities for early years
Responding to stories

Christine Moorcroft
Illustrations by Alison Dexter
Photographs by Zul Mukhida

Contents

A & C Black · London

Introduction

Responding to Stories shows how stories can be used to support all areas of learning for children up to the age of five. It is designed to help teachers of reception and nursery classes, nursery teachers, course leaders, voluntary helpers in nurseries and play-groups – indeed anyone involved with the education of children between the ages of three and five to plan their teaching in an imaginative and thoughtful way.

The stories have been chosen for their appeal to children of this age and for the ways in which they can contribute to the areas of learning identified by SCAA (now QCA) in January 1996 in the *Desirable Outcomes for Children's Learning on Entering Compulsory Education*:

personal and social development, which includes relationships and attitudes to learning, as well as health education;

language and literacy, which is about talk-ing, listening, reading, and using books;

mathematics, which includes understanding of numbers, size, shape, position, patterns, the beginnings of addition and subtraction and the language of number;

knowledge and understanding of the world, in which children learn about where they live, their families, and past and present events in their own lives, about why things happen and how things work, how materials can be used to make things and how computers and other information technology can help them in their work;

physical development, which is about the ways in which children develop physical control and mobility, awareness of space and use of manipulative skills in indoor and outdoor environments;

creative development, which is about developing children's ability to express their ideas and feelings in creative ways: in music, visual arts and words.

Some of the stories included in this book have potential to enhance children's learning in more than one of these areas of learning, for example: activities for language, knowledge and understanding of the world and physical development leap out of *We're Going on a Bear Hunt* by Michael Rosen; *The Very Hungry Caterpillar* by Eric Carle buzzes with ideas for mathematics and science; *My Presents* by Rod Campbell inspires activities to do with language and personal and social development; and *The Train Ride* by June Crebbin is a treasure chest of ideas for knowledge and understanding of the world, and sings with sounds and music.

The author and publisher would like to thank the staff and children of the follow-ing nurseries for their help in carrying out the case-studies and allowing themselves and their work to be photographed:

Sand Dunes Nursery, Seaforth, Merseyside (Sefton LEA)
Greenacre Nursery, Bootle, Merseyside (Sefton LEA).

Each chapter includes observations which were made by the teachers when they reflected on the activities they'd carried out with the children in their nursery settings.

To help teachers with their planning, each chapter has clear learning outcomes; key vocabulary is identified; resources are listed; opportunities for the assessment of children's learning are pointed out; and activities for differentiation and extending children's learning are suggested.

Throughout the book there is an emphasis on the ways in which children can be encouraged to respond to stories, to make up their own stories and to take part in role play. There are ideas for ways in which to present books as a source of enjoyment for the children, to help them to learn to read and begin to appreciate how books are organised.

Part of each chapter provides ideas for involving parents, suggesting ways in which co-operation and two-way communication between school or nursery and parents can enhance children's learning, and recognising the important part which parents can play.

Sometimes it is suggested that teachers buy extra copies of the book so that they can be taken apart for ordering, matching and other activities. This is not as extravagant as it sounds! It turns the books, many of which cost as little as £1.99, into valuable teaching resources which can be used again and again if they are laminated as suggested.

The books suggested are all in print as we go to press. Most of them were bought, or ordered, from high street bookshops. The following, which accept school requisitions, had excellent selections and were particularly helpful:

Broadbents,
5-7 Market Street,
Southport, PR8 1HD.
Tel 01704 532064.
Fax 01704 542009.

Madeleine Lindley,
The Book Centre,
Broadgate,
Chadderton, OL9 9XA.
Tel 0161 683 4400.
Fax 0161 682 6801.

Pritchards Book Shop,
42 Litherland Road,
Crosby,
Liverpool L23 5SF.
Tel 0151 931 1642.

Myself and other people

Responding to: *This is Our House*
by Michael Rosen (Walker Books)

Intended learning

To help the children to establish effective relationships with others by developing their willingness to share things. To develop the children's skills in speaking and listening.

The story

A little boy called George plays house in an enormous cardboard box which he has found in the playground near the high-rise flats where he lives. The other children in the neighbourhood want to play too, but George refuses to let them in: "This house is mine and no one else is coming in!" he insists.

They try to reason with him, to no avail: he guards it fiercely, managing to keep out seven other would-be inhabitants and a dog. Eventually he has to leave the 'house' – to go to the toilet! The others seize their chance and leap in; when George returns they won't let him in, but by now the house is so crowded that it falls apart.

Key vocabulary

belongs, everybody, I, me, mine, ours, share, us, you, yours

The activity

You will need:

an enormous cardboard box; paint and brushes; small off-cuts of carpet; old curtains or oddments of fabric.

Before reading the story

● Ask the children to complete the sentence: 'I/we share...': for example, 'We share our felt-tips', 'I share my ball', 'We share our house'. To encourage them to listen to one another, ask them to make up sentences which describe what others share.

● What do the children share with others in school, with their families at home, and with their friends and families in other places?

● What do the children not like sharing? Why? They could talk about a time when they did not want to share something.

● Show the children a picture of an exciting game, toy, or piece of play equipment (it could be in a big book or mail order or retail catalogue). Ask them who would like to play with it. What would happen if they all tried to play with it at once?

Encourage them to think about arguments, fights, people being hurt and the toy being broken. How could the children make sure that none of these happens? (They could take turns.) Can they think of a way to make this fair, to decide who goes first and to make sure that some children do not have a much longer time than others?

After reading the story

● Talk about what George said when other children came to play in the house, and what the others said to George.

4

Why did George have to go out of the house? Ask the children to retell what happened next. Can they say what George learned at the end of the story?

● Ask the children to retell the story, substituting their own names and the names of their friends for those in the story.

● Help a group of children to make their own 'house': cut out a 'door' and a 'window' out of the biggest cardboard box you can find. Ask the children to choose the colours with which to paint the walls, door and window frame. Once the paint is dry, varnish it; this will not only enhance the appearance of the 'house' but strengthen the cardboard.

● A small group of children could use oddments of fabric to make a carpet and curtains. (The activity could take place in the role-play corner as well as in a 'house' made by the children.)

● Groups of children could take turns to make up a role-play based on the story, using some of the words from the book and/or some of their own. They could practise their 'plays' then perform them for the rest of the class.

The children decided that only four of them could play in the house at one time. They displayed this rule for everyone to read.

Assessment

● Could the children name things which they share with others?

● After listening to the story, were they able to give examples of George's words to the other children in the story?

● Could they remember any of the children's names?

● How well did they work with others in a group?

● Did they offer any ideas to solve practical problems when making the house?

● How well were they able to take turns in telling a story to the others and to listen to others who did the same?

Evidence of the children's learning

Some of the children thought George wanted to keep the others out of the house because it would get too crowded. Some of them recognised that this was not fair: that everyone who wanted to should have a turn in the house. Others said that it was George's house because he found the box. 'George made it,' said one. After discussion, most of the children agreed that George would have more friends if he shared his things.

The children suggested ways in which the children in the story could have shared the house without making it fall apart. We made a list of rules for using the house which we'd set up in the home corner: everyone has a turn to play in it and only four children can play in it at one time. We displayed this sharing rule on a notice in the house.

Differentiating the activity

To help children who have difficulty understanding the concept of sharing, talk about playing together and taking turns to use equipment. The children could share out biscuits, fruit or sweets so that each child in their group has the same number. They could divide up modelling clay or dough into equal-sized pieces for each member of their group.

Provide one toy for a group of two or three children. Ask them who is going to play with the toys whether this is fair and what they could do to make it more fair. Help them to find a picture of something they could share with their friends and to complete a 'sharing' sentence, verbally, for example: 'I share my — with ——'. An adult could write down the completed sentence and read it with the children.

Extension activities

Help the children to tell their own stories in which people won't share with others but learn to share by the end of the story. An adult could transcribe and display their stories with their illustrations, or the children could attempt to write them, then tell them to an adult.

Make 'sharing' flags to display whenever the children help others, take turns or share equipment. Make a class *Sharing* book, displaying labelled photographs of the children sharing equipment, activities, learning and enjoyment with one another.

Involving parents

Invite parents to tell you about anything which the children have shared willingly at home. It might help if a notebook is used, in which parents can write a brief note about their child's sharing activity at home. The notes could be read with the child and/or read aloud to the class.

Other books to use

HELPING ONE ANOTHER

Cleversticks
by Bernard Ashley (Collins Picture Lions)

Ling Sung started school on Monday, but by Wednesday he did not want to go any more, because there were so many things he couldn't do, such as tying shoe laces, writing his name and fastening buttons. But his teacher found something at which he was very clever - eating with chopsticks! Ling Sung teaches the other children (and the teachers) how to use chopsticks, and his friends begin to help him with the things he cannot do.

Ask the children about the things they can do, and what they want to learn to do. Organise a practice time each day when they can help one another with the things they want to learn. Talk about the ways in which the children can help one another, drawing attention to the children's abilities, by asking questions such as 'Who could help you with a drawing?', 'Who could help you to fasten a zip?'

Make a class book or display of photographs showing how the children have helped one another. Keep a diary of how they help one another in the normal course of events each day as a 'reward' for friendly, caring behaviour.

MYSELF, LIKES AND DISLIKES

The Blanket
by John Burningham (Red Fox)

The child in the story (it could be a boy or a girl) cannot find his (or her) special blanket. It is bedtime, and he or she always takes the blanket to bed. There is a full-scale search, accompanied by a few tears and some thumb-sucking. Then the blanket is found - under a pillow. The child goes to sleep, smiling contentedly.

This book is suitable for the youngest children. Ask them about their special things. What do they take to bed with them? Has it ever been lost? How did they feel? What did they do? What did they feel or say when they found it ?

FEELINGS

What's That Noise?
by Francesca Simon & David Melling (Hodder)

Harry, a little rabbit, stays at his grandparents' house. At night he hears noises. Each sound frightens him; he calls his grandfather who comforts him. Then Grandfather hears a snuffling noise. What can it be? He is frightened and calls for Grandma. They creep around the house until they find out what it is - it is Harry snoring! Grandma comforts Grandfather and tucks him into his bed!

Ask the children about noises which they have heard at night. Which scared them? They could describe a time when they were scared. What did they do? What stopped them being scared?

What Makes Me Happy?
by Catherine and Laurence Anholt (Walker)

This book shows children experiencing different feelings and describing what causes them. They describe things which make them laugh or cry and which make them bored, pleased, jealous, scared, sad, excited, shy, cross or happy.

After reading the book, ask the children whether any of the same things make them happy. They could draw pictures of themselves feeling happy. How can they tell when someone is happy? Talk about happy times in the nursery and at home.

I wonder

Responding to: *Why is the Sky Blue?*
by Sally Grindley & Susan Varley
(Andersen Press)

Intended learning

To develop the children's sense of wonder about
the world around them; to encourage them to
ask and answer questions, and to listen to the
person who is speaking.

The story

An elderly donkey wants to share with a young
rabbit the wisdom he has accumulated about
the world, including why the sky is blue.
Donkey scarcely moves from his corner of a
field. He chews grass all day, nodding his head
wisely. Rabbit pops up all over the field, from
different exits from his burrow. He is so
inquisitive that he cannot sit still for long:
instead of listening to the old donkey he is
busy looking at everything around him.

Before each attempt to answer Rabbit's question
('Why is the sky blue?'), Donkey tells him that
he will teach him all he knows - if he will sit
still and listen. Before Donkey gets very far,
Rabbit always has more and more
questions. Donkey sits patiently chewing grass,
waiting for Rabbit to return from racing
around the field.

In the end Rabbit teaches Donkey a new way
of learning (by observation), and works out his
own explanation for the colour of the sky.

Key vocabulary

know, listen, sit still, tell, watch,
why

The activity

You will need:

saucers of ready-mixed paint in primary
colours, green, white, black and brown;
materials with which to print, such as sponges;
blue paper; large paintbrushes; large and
small water-based felt-tips; white art paper and
writing paper; black, yellow and red paper.

Before reading the story

● Tell the children the title of the story and ask
them why *they* think the sky is blue; record their
responses.

● The teacher and/or adult helpers could tell
the children about things which have made
them wonder, for example: why things fall
downwards and not upwards; why eggs have
shells; or why bees buzz.

The children could try to answer these
questions.

● The children could talk about things which
make them wonder. They could try to answer
one another's questions, such as: 'Why is the
sun yellow?', 'Why do dogs bark?' and 'How
can we see big things when our eyes are very
small?' Record their responses.

After reading the story

● Talk about old people the children know who, like the donkey, have accumulated a lot of knowledge. Make a list of the questions the children would like to ask them.

● The children could bring to school, to show and talk about or to display, things which make them wonder, for example: a flower, or a mechanical device such as the inside of a clock or a clockwork toy.

● Take the children outside to look for 'wonderful things', such as: spiders' webs, birds' nests, snowflakes, the patterns of frost, birds singing, or ants working together to collect food. Encourage them to talk about natural wonders, for example: how a spider can walk on its web without sticking to it, how it builds the web; what makes all blackbirds sing the same tune or how snowflakes are made.

● The children could print 'wonderful world' pictures on sky-blue backgrounds. With help, they could cut out red ladybirds, count their spots and fix them onto the background; cut out bees from yellow paper, paint on black stripes and glue on black legs and antennae.

Others could make butterfly shapes by folding a piece of white paper in half, putting splodges of paint on one half, then pressing the two halves together. The children's observational paintings of flowers could be added to the display.

● Make a book in which to record the children's 'wonders', which can be transcribed by an adult and illustrated by the children.

The children looked at pictures of real ladybirds before making a display of their own.

Assessment

● Can the children express some ideas about why the sky is blue?

● Can they talk about other things which make them wonder?

● Do they respond to other children's 'wonders'?

● Do they listen to the person who is speaking?

● Can they talk about things which they or others brought to school?

● Are the children able to describe how the two animals in the story learned?

● Can the children ask questions about things they observe?

● When asked questions, do their replies provide an answer?

Evidence of the children's learning

We told the children that they were going to try to find things out in the same way as the rabbit – by observing and asking questions. We asked them to listen while we showed them a picture book about the solar system and taught them the names of some of the planets. Then we asked them to name the same planets: which was nearest to the Earth and which was nearest to the Sun? The children realised that they had learned the names of the planets.

We talked about the ways in which the children learned about ladybirds - by listening to adults, looking at books and watching real ladybirds very carefully themselves. Some of them could say what they had learned about ladybirds. They then made a display of their own ladybirds including a huge one made from scrunched up tissue paper glued on to a cut-out background.

Differentiating the activity

To help children who have difficulty in asking and answering questions, encourage them to talk about their observations of the world around them; they could point out flowers, trees, birds and 'minibeasts' (this word is used so that small creatures which are not insects can be grouped with insects).

Provide a selection of pictures of living things, about which the children can ask and answer questions with help, for example, 'does it have legs?', 'how many legs does it have?', 'does it have wings?', 'how does it move?' and 'what colour is it?'

Extension activities

Each day provide the children with a new 'I wonder' discussion. The stimulus could be something beautiful (natural or manufactured), like an orchid or a painting; something complicated like a mechanical device; or a picture of something very big, such as an ancient structure like a standing stone circle or the Pyramids, or an enormous building.

I wonder how they got the big stones onto the top?

Involving parents

Encourage parents to look closely, with their children, at the things which they see around them; can they find anything which they had not noticed before, like the old donkey noticing how bees collect pollen?

Communication with parents can be arranged via a notebook, which the children could become accustomed to taking home. They could write a sentence in the notebook to describe something new which they and the child have noticed.

Other books to use

Heaven
by Nicholas Allan (Hutchinson)

This story features a little girl whose dog has been invited to heaven by a couple of angels, who collect him with his suitcase from the churchyard. It explores ideas about heaven: where it is and what it is like. It also shows how people might feel when someone they love dies.

The book shows a connection between death and heaven by having gravestones in the churchyard from which the dog is taken by the angels (they come to meet him and carry him, with his suitcase, up into the sky).

Do the children know what the things in the picture are? Why are there gravestones in a churchyard? Why is the dog going to heaven? Can the children explain why Lily cannot go with him?

Ask the children what they think about heaven. Where is it? Who is in it?

What would be their idea of a perfect place? They could paint pictures of it.

Who Can Tell?
by Stuart Henson (Hutchinson)

A little boy leaves food on the doorstep to encourage badgers to come from the woods into his garden. The story describes what he sees, wonders and dreams as he waits late into the night and hopes to see the badgers, for example: 'Who can tell what the trees say when they whisper among themselves at the end of the day?'

Have the children ever stayed up late at night, waiting, and hoping to see something special: Father Christmas on Christmas Eve, perhaps, or a nocturnal animal such as a badger?

How did they feel? What did they do while they were waiting? Talk about the seemingly long time of waiting.

The Tiny Seed
by Eric Carle (Puffin)

It is autumn and seeds are being carried by the wind. One by one, many of them are destroyed. Somehow the tiniest seed survives all the dangers it meets on its travels until, at last, it lands on some snow-covered earth. There it stays until spring. What will happen to it? All the other seeds have begun to grow, but some of the plants die. Then the tiny seed begins to grow into a plant. A child runs past, trampling another plant underfoot, but still the tiny seed grows. Eventually it grows into an enormous flower. Seeds grow in it. Then, in the autumn, the story starts again...

Show the children some seeds and the flowers or fruits which grow from them. Show them acorns, chestnuts, beech nuts and horse chestnuts and pictures of the trees which grow from them (or, better still, the real thing). How can these big plants grow from such tiny seeds? How did the land on Earth become covered with plants of different kinds? The children could draw pictures to make into a book of 'wonders of nature'.

Celebrating

Responding to: *Happy Birthday Sam*
by Pat Hutchins (Picture Puffins)

Intended learning

For the children to appreciate the feeling of celebration and to recognise that celebrations commemorate events; for them to begin to understand the idea of regularly recurring celebrations. For the children to begin to develop the understanding that messages can be written to be read again.

The story

It is Sam's birthday; he is a whole year older! He jumps out of bed to see if he is now big enough to turn on the light by himself, and reach the clothes in his wardrobe and the taps in the bathroom. But he is no bigger than he was the day before – he still can't reach them!

Then the post arrives: there is an enormous parcel for Sam. It is a special present from his grandfather – a little chair which is just the right size for Sam, and on which he can stand to reach the light switches, the clothes in his wardrobe, the taps, and many other things.

Being able to do things by himself makes Sam's birthday special, particularly when Grandpa arrives and Sam can reach the door knob, open the door and let him in – all by himself.

Key vocabulary

birthday, five, four, happy, older, one, party, reach, three, two, year

The activity

You will need:

brightly-coloured display paper, glue, white art paper, cookery magazines and brochures showing pictures of birthday cakes, a teddy bear, a calendar which has large clear numbers and text, cake ingredients, baking equipment, oven, scissors, gift wrapping, used birthday cards, art straws, masking tape.

Before reading the story

● Do the children know that a birthday is the date on which someone was born? Do they know the dates of their own birthdays? Help them to find the dates on a calendar. How old are they now, and how old will they be on their next birthday? Do they know how often they have a birthday?

● Ask the children to describe some of the special things they do on their birthdays. What do they do on birthdays to make them different from ordinary days?

● Talk about the children's favourite birthday presents: what was special about them?

● To whom have the children given birthday presents? They could talk about the presents they have chosen for members of their families and for friends. How did they decide what to give them?

After reading the story

● Make a class birthday book, allocating a large page for each month. Ask the children to draw and label a picture of themselves and to glue it onto the square for their own birthdays. Adults connected with the school could add their pictures and names to the book.

The children could check the book each day to see if anyone's birthday is on the next day.

● Take a teddy bear into the nursery or class and tell the children that he is going to have a birthday (show the date on a calendar). Ask the children what they could do to help Teddy celebrate his birthday. They could draw their ideas, which could be annotated by an adult.

● Ask the children to help you make a cake for Teddy's birthday. Talk about the ways in which a birthday cake can be made to look different from ordinary cakes. How can the children make Teddy's cake special? How many candles will it have?

● Ask the children to decide how they can prepare the classroom for Teddy's birthday party. They could make paper chains, 'happy birthday' banners and write birthday messages. Talk about the purpose of these messages: for someone else to read.

● The children can choose birthday cards for Teddy. Ask them to explain their choices, which can be displayed. They could make their own birthday cards and address them to Teddy.

We planned and held a birthday party for Teddy.

Assessment

● Do the children know the month of their birthday?

● Do they know that this month comes every year and that they are then one year older?

● Can the children talk about some of the ways in which people celebrate birthdays and other events?

● Can they name other events which they celebrate?

● Can the children write, in their own way, a birthday message and then read what they have written?

Evidence of the children's learning

Most of the children could find their birthday months on a calendar; some of them could also find the date. We talked about the things to which the children look forward to being able to do when they are older, such as being allowed to stay up as late as their older siblings, and watch particular programmes on television.

The children collected pictures of birthday cakes and chose the one they liked best, giving the reasons for their choice. 'I don't like this one, it's got too much icing on it,' said one girl. 'I like this one because it looks like a train,' said another.

They helped to make a birthday cake for Teddy. Some of them were able to help with weighing and measuring the ingredients. The children made cards for Teddy and copied the words 'Happy Birthday' on to them. We set up a party table and sang 'happy birthday' to Teddy. The children took turns to offer Teddy the party food and drink we'd put on the table.

Differentiating the activities

To help children who have difficulty in understanding the idea of celebration, provide pictures of party hats from which the children can choose a design which they like. Talk about the materials from which they can make their hats and how they can join the materials. Help them to make their chosen designs.

Ask them how it makes them feel when they wear their party hats? (Does it feel like an ordinary school day? How do the hats make it special?)

Extension activities

Help the children to make a 'happy birthday train', to show all their birthdays (and Teddy's birthday).

The children could help to draw and cut out the trucks and engine; some might be able to write the names of the months on the sides of the trucks. Ask them to draw and cut out their faces (with happy smiles) from stiff paper or thin card and to attach them with masking tape to an art straw. Can they put them into the trucks which show the months of their birthdays?

Involving parents

Parents could help their child to recognise the month of his or her birthday and possibly to copy it. They could show them the actual date and help the child to copy this number. Encourage parents to talk to their children about birthday presents and cards which would be suitable for people they know.

Other books to use

My Presents
by Rod Campbell (Campbell Books)

This is a story about a birthday party: the reader opens the presents after trying to work out what is inside each box, as its contents are described. On each left-hand page we are told who gave the present, and on each facing page there is a flap consisting of a wrapped present with a tag which shows who gave it. Beneath this the present is described, for example: 'They are all different colours. I like building with them.' The children lift or pull down the flaps to find out what is inside the parcels (in the example it is a set of building blocks).

Wrap a toy in children's birthday gift-wrapping paper and tie a bow and label onto it. Ask the children what they can tell one another about the parcel. How do they know it contains a present? Is it for a child or a grown-up? How can they tell?

Talk about the times when they give and receive presents. What is special about these times? What else do they do at these special times? The children could describe the ways in which these special days are different from other days.

Talk about the ways in which the children might prepare for a special day: what might they do and wear? They could enact a special day of their choice.

Kim's Magic Tree
by Verna Allette Wilkins (Tamarind)

Christmas is over...or is it? The Christmas tree is just as reluctant as Kim to end the festive time. It is a magic tree which grows a big smile and a pair of feet on which it runs away after promising Kim it will be back if she says the magic words. Back it comes, complete with lights which shine without the help of electricity. It can do all sorts of useful tasks like dusting and polishing, cleaning and tidying.

Talk about the end of any celebration: how do the children feel at the end of a party? What do they do to try to make Christmas (or any other celebration) last? Do they keep anything to remind them of it? They could make up their own 'magic' stories.

The children could colour and cut out pictures of individual fairy lights to glue on to a 'magic Christmas tree' collage. They could copy and complete 'fairy light' sequences in which they need to notice the colours of the lights and/or their shapes.

The Magical Bicycle
by Berlie Doherty and Christian Birmingham (Collins Picture Lions)

A little boy opens his presents. The best surprise of all is a bicycle, but he cannot ride it. He falls off every time he tries. He bruises his knees and bangs his chin. His big brother can ride it. Everyone else seems to be able to ride a bicycle. There has to be a special magic trick to it. Then, at last, he learns the magic trick - at last he can ride it!

Talk about presents the children have had which have given them a challenge, such as a bicycle, roller blades, a book. How did they feel when they were presented with something that seemed too difficult for them? Can they describe how they felt when, at last they were able to skate, ride or read?

Keeping healthy

Responding to: *Avocado Baby*
by John Burningham (Red Fox)

Intended learning

To introduce the idea that the food people eat
has an effect on their health, and to encourage
the children to try 'new' foods. To begin to use
conventions of story language in retelling
stories.

The story

Mr and Mrs Hargraves and their two children
are very weak. They hope that their new baby
will be strong; but no, the baby, too, turns out
to be weak, disliking any food offered – except
avocado pear.

The avocado diet endows the baby with super-
human strength; the story goes on to describe
some amazing feats by the baby, such as
rescuing big brother and sister from two
bullies, and throwing a burglar out of the
house.

Key vocabulary

**avocado, baby, eat, no, flesh,
pip, seed, skin, stone, strong,
weak, yes**

The activity

You will need:

packets of baby foods, photographs of a
mother breast-feeding a baby and a mother
(and, if possible, a father too) bottle-feeding
a baby; an avocado, a plate and a knife;
examples of other fruits, pictures of fruits and
other foods; magazines from which the
children can cut pictures of food; scissors, glue,
paper, paper plates, dough made from flour
and water with some salt and food colourings
added.

Before reading the story

● Talk about foods for babies: on what are
new-born babies fed?

● What sorts of foods do babies soon begin to
eat? Why? The children should have noticed
that babies have no teeth, which means that
they cannot chew. Explain to them that babies'
stomachs can only manage foods without
strong flavours.

● If possible, ask a mother to bring her baby
into the class for a feed, and to talk about
baby-feeding.

● Show the children pictures of foods and a
picture of a six-month-old baby, and ask what
the baby could or could not eat, for example:
chips, a carrot, milk, canned baby food, steak,
curry, a packet of baby cereal – and an
avocado. Record their responses on a big chart:

● Tell the children the title of the story and ask
them if they have seen an avocado before.
Have they ever tasted one? Can they say the
word 'avocado'? They could practise this
together.

Right: We examined an avocado, described it and then cut it open so that the children could taste it.
They were surprised at the size of the stone. Then we talked about whether a six-month old
baby would be able to eat the flesh of an avocado. One child then placed the cut avocado
onto the appropriate section of the chart we'd made.

After reading the story

● Talk about the Hargraves family; can the children say why they think the family members are weak? The children could give their ideas about what strong people can do, and how weak people are different.

● Ask the children to sort a set of pictures of foods into the categories 'fruit' and 'not fruit'.

● With flour and water dough, the children could make models of their 'favourite meals' and arrange them on paper plates.

● Show the children an avocado. Do they know what it is like inside? Cut it open and show them. Do they know the names of the different parts of the fruit? Point out the skin, flesh and stone. Give each child a small piece to taste. Do they like it? Tell them it is a fruit, and ask them to name other fruits.

● The children could tell their own stories about 'magic' foods. They could draw pictures to illustrate their stories which could be transcribed by an adult.

The Magic Apple

Once upon a time a little girl and her mother were walking down the street when they met a mysterious woman who was selling apples. By mistake the little girl picked out the magic apple. At first she did not know that it was magic. They took it home. The little girl took a bite out of the magic apple. Suddenly there was a clatter and somebody knocked at the door. He gave the child and her mother eight sacks full of gold. They lived happily ever after.

Assessment

● Can the children give examples of suitable foods for babies?

● Can they make up a simple story about a magic food?

● Do they know the names of familiar fruits and can they identify them?

● Do they talk about the foods they like and dislike?

● Can they describe in simple terms one reason for which we need food? (For example 'to make us grow strong'.)

Evidence of the children's learning

Some of the children could say why Mrs Hargraves was worried about the new baby, and why was this baby was so weak. They were eager to talk about what happened after the baby began to eat avocado and had mixed ideas as to whether this could really happen: 'It was a magic avocado.';
'The baby isn't in real life.'

All the children knew that babies are fed on milk. Some of them could identify fruits in a collection of foods; others needed help. A few knew that fruits contain seeds. One girl said that her brother had once swallowed a plum stone. All the children could find pictures of food they like (and of food they didn't like!) and could complete (orally) the sentence:
'I like to eat...'.

They made a 'healthy foods' scrap-book with pictures of foods which help us to grow strong, such as meat, fish, dairy products, beans and pulses and grains.

Differentiating the activity

To help the children with a limited vocabulary of the names of foods, encourage them to talk about foods they like. Make cards showing labelled pictures of fruits; show them and read them to the children, and then ask them to find fruits which you nominate. Do the same with other kinds of food.

Extension activities

Set up a class greengrocery shop in which the children can buy and sell replica fruit and vegetables. Provide a toy till or a box containing plastic money, paper and a pen for writing 'customers' orders' and a collection of imitation fruit and vegetables.

With adult help, the children could examine a collection of fruits, including an avocado: they could identify those with smooth, rough, or bumpy skins; they could sort them according to colour or size. Cut open the fruits and ask the children which have thick and which have thin skins; which have tiny seeds, which have pips and which have stones; which have just one of these and which have a lot of them?

Involving parents

Encourage parents to talk to their children about their food likes and dislikes. While shopping they could talk about the foods they see on supermarket shelves, asking the children to find the fruits.

In school, the children could name the fruits they remember seeing. They could each draw a fruit which an adult could help them to label. Display the fruits in a 'fruit bowl'.

Other books to use

Jack's Tummy
by Katharine McEwen (Chart Books)

This story describes a little boy who eats things he shouldn't. Eventually he is very spectacularly SICK. At last he heeds his mother's advice and eats proper food. There is a picture of him eating a healthy meal.

Talk about the dangers of eating things which might be dangerous. Do the children know of anyone who has had to go to hospital because he or she swallowed something dangerous? Ask the children about times when they have been sick; how did they feel, who looked after them, and what made them feel better?

Handa's Surprise
by Eileen Browne (Walker Books)

Handa, who lives in Kenya, chooses seven fruits which she puts in a basket for her friend Akeyo. She carries the flat basket of fruit on her head as she walks to Akeyo's village. As Handa wonders which fruit Akeyo likes best, thinking of them each in turn, an animal steals it from the basket. As it does so the fruit is described. Eventually the basket is empty. Then Handa passes a tree which is butted by a goat. Out of the tree falls a shower of tangerines. They land in the basket. What a surprise for Handa, as well as for Akeyo, when Handa arrives at Akeyo's village!

Provide samples of the fruits named in the story, for the children to examine and taste. Which have they tasted before? Which are new to them? The children could draw one of the new fruits they tried and say whether or not they liked it.

The children could enact the story using a real basket and fruits. Can they remember the order in which the fruits were taken from the basket and which animal stole them?

A Birthday Cake for Little Bear
by Max Velthuijs (North-South Books)

Little Pig decides to bake a birthday cake for Little Bear. The appetising smell of baking wafts through the neighbourhood; first Duck and then Rabbit follow the smell to Little Pig's house. The cake looks so delicious they offer to taste it: 'If you give someone a present you have to be sure it's good.' Little Pig adjusts the flavouring of the cream and they have to taste it again, to be sure that it is right. Just in time, Little Bear calls to find out what the lovely smell is. A small piece is all that's left of his cake. 'We had to taste it to make sure it was good,' say the other animals, 'but you can have the only bit with some strawberries and cream left on it.'

Rather than labelling all sweet foods 'unhealthy', talk to the children about foods for special occasions. Explain that eating too many foods which contain a lot of sugar can harm our teeth, and that eating too many foods which have a lot of fat and sugar in them can make people fat, but to eat them once in a while does no harm. If possible, make a cake with the children for a special occasion, such as the last day of term.

Bread and Jam for Frances
by Russell and Lillian Hoban (Picture Puffins)

Frances likes bread and jam so much that she eats it for every meal. One day when everyone else in the family is offered spaghetti and meatballs, Frances is given bread and jam, because she has always refused to eat anything else. She begins to realise what she is missing and cries. She asks if she can have some spaghetti and meatballs and, to her mother's amazement, she eats it all up.

Talk about the times when the children have refused to eat a meal. They could talk about their feelings, any arguments with adults at home, and what happened in the end. Do they know why people at home encourage them to eat certain foods?

Patterns and rhymes

Responding to:
We're Going on a Bear Hunt
by Michael Rosen (Walker Books)

Intended learning

To help the children to enjoy stories and to develop their ability to associate sounds with words, to recognise repeated words and to retell a story.

The story

A family goes for a walk: parents, a little boy, a little girl, a baby and a dog. The story is told, as if by one of the children, in a way which blurs the distinctions between imagination and reality and invites the questions, 'Was it really a bear hunt?' and 'Was there really a bear?'.

The family in the story apparently cross an obstacle course, until they reach a dark cave, in which they meet a bear. They retrace their steps, rush into their home, close the door just in time to keep out the bear, and hide where all children feel safe – under the bedclothes. Each page repeats some of the words of the previous page in a way which encourages the children to join in.

Key vocabulary

bear, hunt, over, through, under

The activity

You will need:

construction material; recycled materials; a cassette recorder and a cassette; thin raffia in long pieces, thin strips of plastic or a door-curtain made from strips of plastic (as used by some food shops in the summer); cornflour; bowls; a water tray; dolls or small model people.

Before reading the story

● Ask the children if they have ever set out on an adventure. They could talk about days out, or holidays.

● With whom did they go? Where did they go, and what were they looking for? They could talk about times when they have explored places like woodland, parks or beaches.

● The children could describe adventures in which they have pretended that familiar places and things were something else.

● Have they ever found anything which scared them? This might be something which just startles them and which they found was not really frightening after all, such as a strange noise or a sudden movement or perhaps a shadow. How did the children feel and what did they do when they discovered that it was not really frightening after all?

● The children could use model people or dolls to help them to tell an adventure story, recreating the scene using everyday classroom equipment such as boxes, cardboard or cardboard tubes. They could use puppets to help tell their stories.

After reading the story

● Talk about the words which are repeated in the story, and ask the children if they can remember them. Encourage them to continue when you stop at any point, for example:

'We're going on a bear hunt.
We're going to catch a big one.
What a beautiful day.
We're not scared.'

● Talk about the sounds made by the obstacles which the family crossed (for example, 'swishy, swashy', 'hooo, woooo') and the characters' actions as they did so (for example, 'stumble, trip', 'tiptoe, tiptoe').

● After practising reading the words 'swishy, swashy', 'splish, splosh', and 'squelch, squerch', a small group of children could find things with which to make those sounds. They could perform these while the rest of the class say the appropriate 'sound' words. Display the objects they used, labelled with the 'sound words' they represent.

● A small group of children could use everyday classroom construction material and recycled materials to construct the places through which the people in the story travelled and to trace their journey. They could move dolls or small model characters through the obstacles as they take turns to retell parts of the story to one another.

We covered a cardboard box with cut-up bin liners to make a 'bear cave'. The children took turns to be the 'bear' in the cave and to frighten away the others.

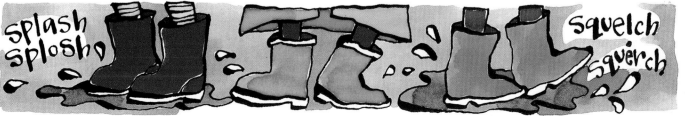

splash splosh   squelch squerch

Assessment

● Can the children talk about their own real or imaginary adventures?

● Can they join in with the repeated words in the story?

● Are they able to continue these if the reader stops?

● Can the children think of words to describe their own sounds or actions?

● Can they make up words for sounds and actions?

● Can the children make sounds which are described to them?

Evidence of the children's learning

The children were able to think of other obstacles they might have to cross during an adventure. They pretended to cross them and made the sounds. They thought of words to describe their actions (at first the children need-ed some direction); we asked them to pretend they were crossing: a sandy beach, big rocks, a jungle, a busy road, a high wall, a thunder-storm. As they did, they repeated the words of the story, changing them (with help) as appro-priate and using words to describe their actions or the sounds around them, for example:

'Uh-uh! A sandy beach!
A hot, soft sandy beach!
We can't go over it.
We can't go under it.
Oh no!
We've got to go through it.'

'Plod crunch! Plod crunch! Plod crunch!'

Differentiating the activity

To help the children to use descriptive words, make a 'bear hunt' corner in the classroom, through which the children can move while they listen to and describe the sounds and their actions.

The 'swishy swashy' part could be made from thin raffia suspended from wooden struts attached to the tops of display boards which meet at right angles, or you could use a curtain made from strips of plastic; 'splish splosh' could be provided by a bowl of water or a water tray; for 'squelch squerch' you could use a bowl containing a thick mixture of cornflour and water, possibly coloured with food dye.

Label each 'sound area' and encourage the children to think of some of their own to add to it. Provide aprons or overalls.

Extension activities

Provide a group of children with a tape recording of, for example: high heels tapping on hard ground, someone slurping a drink through a straw, birds singing, rustling leaves. The children could think of their own words to describe the sounds. The words can be real or the children's own 'made-up' words. An adult could transcribe what the children say for display next to the objects used to make the sounds.

The children could contribute to a class '*Sound words*' book containing words for sounds accompanied by illustrations or pictures cut from catalogues or magazines.

Some children might be able to write and illustrate their own 'bear hunt' stories.

Involving parents

Encourage parents to talk to their children about sounds in the environment, such as the sounds of twittering birds, meowing or purring cats, barking dogs, rustling leaves and muttering voices. They could encourage the children to make up words which describe the sounds.

Provide a notebook in which parents can write down the sounds they've discussed with their child and make a note of any words the child has invented to describe the sounds they've heard.

Other books to use

This is the Bear
by Sarah Hayes and Helen Craig (Walker Books)

This is the tale of a teddy bear which a dog pushes into a bin. The bin is then emptied into a truck and taken to the rubbish dump. The little boy who owns the teddy tries to find it, helped by his dog and one of the workers at the rubbish dump. The happy ending shows a clean, washed teddy bear who asks his owner to promise not to tell anyone about their adventures – and then asks him in the middle of the night when they can have another day out. The book is written in pairs of rhyming sentences or phrases; one per page.

Read the story to the children while showing them the pictures and inviting them to finish the sentences, for example:

'This is the bear who fell in the (bin).
This is the dog who pushed him (in).'

Ask the children to think of words which rhyme with those which you name, beginning with some from the story. The children could try to think of their own pairs of rhyming words.

Noisy Farm
by Rod Campbell (Picture Puffins)

In this 'lift-the-flap' book, the farm wakes up with the sound of the rooster. 'Cock-a-doodle-doo!' and then the dog barks, 'Woof! Woof!'. There are many more noises to be heard as the reader follows Sam the dog on his journey of discovery around the farm.

Each double-page spread ends with a question about a sound whose source is discovered when the page is turned: for example, 'Sam can hear a chugging noise. What can that be?' Over the page is a picture of a tractor, with the answer, 'It's the tractor off to plough the fields'. There are also questions which begin 'Where is...?' or 'Where are...?', the answers to which can be found by lifting flaps.

The book also shows each animal with its young: the children can learn the names for the young of a sheep, cow, pig, hen and duck.

While reading the story to the children, invite them to answer the question at the end of each right-hand page: they can say what it is which might make each sound, and then turn the page to see if they are right. They could take turns to predict and find out what is under each flap.

After reading the story, ask what makes particular sounds: for example, 'What chugs?', 'What moos?', 'What clucks?' and 'What quacks?'. The children could each make a page for a big 'lift-the-flap' book about animals and their sounds - farm animals, zoo animals or pets (perhaps a pet shop). Help them to make up questions and answers in the style of those in *Noisy Farm*.

splash
splosh

squelch
squerch

Words for describing things

Responding to: *My Presents*
by Rod Campbell (Campbell Books)

Intended learning

To develop vocabulary for describing the appearances and purposes of everyday things, and for the children to recognise and write their own names and those of some of their friends, and the words 'to' and 'from'.

The story

This is a book about a birthday party and presents. Each left-hand page has only the words '... (Name) gave me a/some ... (blank)'. The opposite page shows, on a flap, a wrapped present with a tag which shows who gave it. Beneath this is a description of the present and how it is used, for example: 'They are all different colours. I like painting with them.' The inside of the parcel is revealed by lifting or pulling down the flap (in the example it is a paint-box).

Key vocabulary

birthday, gave, I like, party, presents

The activity

You will need:

cardboard boxes, such as shoe boxes and cartons from cereals, tea and other foods; gift-wrapping paper, gift tags, sticky tape, scissors and items to wrap as gifts; used birthday cards and photographs of people the children know; card and felt-tips, mail-order catalogues and magazines.

Before reading the story

● Ask the children what they did on their last birthday.

● They could describe their presents.

● What was their favourite present? They could say what they liked about it.

● Have the children been to anyone else's birthday party?

● Did they buy a present for him or her?

● What was it?

● If they could buy whatever they wanted for someone they love, what would it be? Why would it be a good present for that person? Record their responses.

● The children could take turns to choose a familiar classroom item which they place behind a screen (the others must not see it). They describe the item to the group or class, who have to work out what it is.

● Help them to do this, if necessary, by asking them to say something about its size ('Is it big, small or in-between?'), its shape ('Is it long, or square, or round or another shape?'), its colour and what it feels like ('Is it hard or soft?', 'Is it rough or smooth?'). Encourage them to use words like: fluffy, shiny and bumpy. They could say what they do with each item.

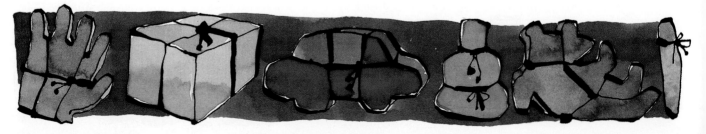

After reading the story

● Ask the children to match some of the words in the book to the presents which they describe, for example:

'He's big and furry.
I like cuddling him!'

'It's round and bouncy.
I like catching it!'

● They could then try to describe a present they have received, in the same way.

● The children could take turns to describe the presents in the book, and say what the child in the story likes doing with it, for example: 'What is the jigsaw puzzle like?' ('It has lots of pieces. I like putting it together.')

● Provide each child in a group with a card on which is a photograph of someone they know (requested from home in advance), with that person's name written in a way which the child can copy or trace. Ask the children to choose a present they think the person would like, cut out a picture of it and glue it below the photograph. They could talk to one another about their choices.

We made a display of presents which the children had wrapped and labelled.

● A group of children could make birthday cards for people they know. Provide used cards from which they can copy birthday messages, including the words: 'to', 'from', and 'happy birthday'. Show the children how to fold card or paper in half and how to know which half (and which way around) to use as the front, on which they should draw a picture of something they think the recipient will like.

Assessment

● Can the children describe the size, shape, feel and purpose of everyday classroom items?

● Can they talk about birthday parties?

● Can they say what they have bought for people's birthdays and describe presents which they themselves have received?

● Having listened to the description of a present in the story, can they predict what will be under the flap?

● Can they explain why a particular present or card would be suitable for someone they know?

● How well do they copy the words 'to' and 'from'? (Do they include any recognisable letters?)

Evidence of children's learning

The children could use the words 'big' and 'small' or 'little' to describe everyday classroom items. A few of them could say, 'It is bigger than a...' and 'It is smaller than a ...'. One of them said that a ruler was long and flat and another said that a pencil was long and round.

The children looked at the gift tags on the presents in the book, to find out who had given them, and some of them were able to recognise the word 'from'.

The children wrapped 'presents'. They each chose a present from a collection of toys and other 'gift' items and then choose a box of the right size in which to pack it. They needed help to cut a piece of wrapping paper of a suitable size for wrapping the present. After wrapping the presents they wrote gift tags: 'From ... (their own name).'

Differentiating the activity

To help children who do not recognise that text consists of separate words, provide the large gift tags made from pictures cut from used birthday cards. Help them to practise writing 'from', then ask them to write 'from' and their name on the tag. Ask them to read what they have written.

Show them how to punch a hole in the tag and then attach a piece of ribbon to it. They could each cut out a rectangle or square of gift-wrapping paper and glue strips of coloured paper onto it (to represent ribbon) to make a two-dimensional collage of a present. Display their tags and gift wrapping paper.

The children could trace or copy sentences which begin 'I like...'. Point out each separate word as they read it.

Extension activities

With the help of an adult the children could choose an item from a collection of 'presents' (toys, games, a plant, bath oil, and so on). They should say what the present is like, for example (a plant): 'It has green leaves and red flowers.' They should then say what they might do with it, for example (plant): 'I like to water it and smell it.' An adult could transcribe the children's responses, to be displayed alongside the 'presents'.

The children could sort used birthday cards (include those featuring flowers, toys, country scenes, party things such as balloons and paper hats, ages and traditional 'male' and 'female' cards) and glue them onto a chart to show for whom they are suitable, for example: Mum, Dad, Grandma, Grandpa, Teacher (teacher's name), Baby. Talk about their choices.

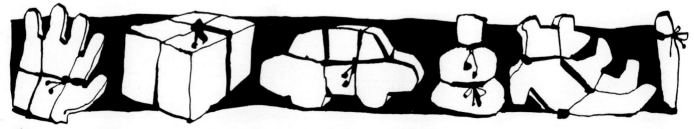

Involving parents

Encourage parents to talk to their children about any presents which they buy, including how they are making the choice; the children could help them to choose. They could also help them to choose birthday cards and gift-wrapping paper, to write in the cards and on the gift tags, and to wrap the presents.

Other books to use

Don't Forget the Bacon
by Pat Hutchins (Picture Puffins)

This is the tale of a little boy who goes shopping for his mother. He tries to remember what she has asked him to buy by repeating the list, but he is distracted by things he sees on the way to the shops. He buys all the wrong things; then on the way home he sees things which remind him what he should have bought, and so he exchanges them, until he has all the right things – except the bacon.

On each double-page spread one item in the list changes. Ask the children to listen carefully and to say what has changed, for example:

'Six farm eggs,
a cake for tea,
a pound of pears,
and don't forget the bacon.'

changes, when the little boy sees a row of women's legs, to:

'Six fat legs,
a cake for tea,
a pound of pears,
and don't forget the bacon.'

In pairs or small groups the children could make up shopping lists of up to four items, and then exchange each item one by one, for something with which it rhymes.

Do You Want To Be My Friend?
by Eric Carle (Picture Puffins)

The only words in this book are on the first page: 'Do you want to be my friend?'. A little mouse is looking for a friend, and it considers each animal it meets as a possible friend. Only part of each animal is shown on a right-hand page of the book - its tail! The rest is revealed as the page is turned. Along the bottom of each page runs, continuously through the book, a long green strip. It could be grass, but is it? The answer is revealed on the penultimate page, after which the mouse finds another mouse to be its friend.

Ask the children to describe each animal's tail which appears on a right-hand page: 'What colour is it?', 'Is it hairy?', 'Is it smooth or bumpy?', 'Is it long or short?', 'Does it have feathers?', 'Does it have scales?'. Can the children work out to which animal each description belongs?

Buster's Day
by Rod Campbell (Campbell Books)

The book describes the activities of a little boy, from when he gets up until he goes to bed. This is another book with flaps for the children to lift after they have predicted what is beneath them. Below each picture with a flap is a question which asks the children what they can see, for example; 'What can you see in the washing machine?', 'What can you see in the kitchen cupboard?'

Ask the children to name the things which they see in each picture. They could make their own pictures with flaps and ask, or perhaps write, 'What can you see...?' questions. Collect their pictures and questions to make a book entitled 'What can you see?'

Time

Responding to: *Time to get up* by Gill McLean (Tamarind) and *Time for Bed* by Alexis Obi (Tamarind)

Intended learning

For the children to be able to put a series of events in the right order and to develop their understanding of time. For the children to be able to tell a story about a series of pictures.

The stories

Time to get up begins at 7.30 am. Anna's father gets up, looking tired, and goes to wake Anna, who does not want to get up ('Not yet, Dad. I'm thinking.') Dad staggers downstairs, yawning, to make a cup of tea. At 7.45 he goes back to make sure Anna is up. 'Not yet, Dad, ' she says, 'I'm reading.' Dad continues getting ready for work, popping back to check on Anna, who seems to have no intention of getting ready to go to school. At 8.25 Dad is ready for work and he insists that she gets ready for school quickly. But she has a very good reason for not doing so - it is Saturday!

Time for Bed is about Kieran, who is very good at postponing bed-time and has toys which seem to be alive. At last his mother persuades him to choose a bed-time story, but he wants to read it to *her*. During the story she falls asleep and Kieran and his toys play happily until they, too, fall asleep.

Key vocabulary

afternoon, get up, late, moon, morning, o'clock, stars, sun, time

The activity

You will need:

two copies of the book, from which pictures can be cut; cardboard clock faces, a collection of clocks and watches; card, painting materials, scissors, glue; role-play corner items.

Before reading the stories

● Talk about mornings. What do the children do in the morning? What sounds do they hear? What do they see happening in and around their homes? For example, do they hear birds singing, or milk, newspapers and post being delivered? Do they hear people setting off for work or for school?

● Talk about getting up. Who or what wakes the children? They could describe what happens when they first wake. Do they get up right away? The children could talk about what they do once they are up: washing, getting ready for school, playing and perhaps watching television. What do their parents do in the morning? What kinds of things do they say to the children?

● Talk about time. Do the children know what time they get up? Do they know what time school starts? They could find out. What time do the children go to bed?

● Talk about bed-time. Do the children get ready for bed as soon as they are told to? What do they do instead? What do they do to try to stay up later than they are supposed to? They could describe the sequence of events before bed-time: for example, watching television, washing, changing, reading a story, having a drink, saying prayers, kissing goodnight.

● Talk about what the grown-ups in the family are doing when the children have to go to bed. What do the children see, hear and smell going on inside and outside their homes?

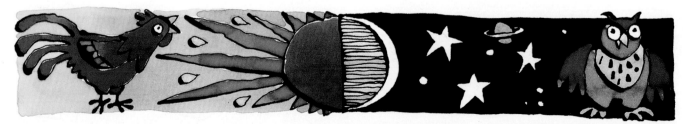

After reading the stories

● Talk about what Anna does in *Time to get up*. Ask the children to look at the pictures cut from two spare copies of the book and arrange them in the order in which matches the sequence of events in the story. The number of pictures used can vary according to the children's age and ability. Do the same with *Time for Bed*.

● The children could paint 'Morning' and 'Night-time' (outdoor) pictures to be displayed against sky blue and dark blue backgrounds respectively. Include a large sun or moon and stars, as appropriate, in the displays. On each display there could be a clock face which shows the time at which most of the children get up or go to bed.

The children helped to choose and cut out pictures from magazines and catalogues which were used to make a display of morning and night-time activities.

● The children could make a collage out of cut out pictures of people doing 'morning' activities, and of things associated with morning, for example, a sunrise, breakfast cereals, a toaster, people eating breakfast, or someone reading a morning newspaper. Similarly, a 'night-time' collage could include the moon and stars, street lamps, pyjamas, night-dresses, or people having supper.

● Help the children to make 'concertina' books which they can illustrate with drawings of their morning and evening routines. Talk about a routine as a repeated sequence of events.

Assessment

● Can the children describe morning and night-time outdoor scenes?

● Can they name some of the things they observe happening around them in the morning and at night?

● Are they able to sequence a set of pictures showing events from the stories?

● Can they, using pictures as prompts, re-tell the main events in one or both of the stories?

● Do their 'concertina' books show their own morning or evening routines in a logical order?

● Do they select appropriate pictures to cut out to represent 'morning' and 'night-time' in collages?

● Can they recognise and show the times, on clocks, at which they get up or go to bed?

Evidence of the children's learning

At first most of the children began describing their own morning and evening routines at random points, adding to it as they remembered what to do. Some of them could do this after sequencing pictures of other children getting up or going to bed, while others needed to practice putting the actions in order using dolls and soft toys.

The children could sequence a set of up to six pictures from each of the stories while looking at the books. After practice, most of them could do this while the stories were being read to them.

The children were then able to use their sequenced pictures as props with which to re-tell the stories to partners.

Differentiating the activity

Children who have difficulty in relating activities to times of the day, and in describing a sequence of activities, could, each morning, set up a role-play corner to show dolls and teddy bears performing different parts of their morning routines. Ask them what the dolls and teddy bears in the role-play corner are doing.

Before they go home they could change it to represent 'night-time'. In the role-play corner the children could enact their own morning and night-time routines while talking about them to one another, or they could prepare the dolls and teddy bears for bed or 'get them up' in the morning.

Extension activities

Provide a collection of clocks for the children to look at and some on which they can change the time: alarm clocks, old watches, clock radios, mantelpiece clocks, toy clocks and cardboard clock faces.

The children could draw pictures to show what time they get up and go to bed. They could draw a clock on their picture with the hands showing this time, and write a caption ('I get up at ... o'clock', 'I go to bed at ... o'clock').

Involving parents

Ask parents to talk about the hour (o'clock) as they carry out some activities with the children, for example: making or eating a meal, watching a favourite television programme, going to bed. They could point out clocks at home and in other places which show 'o'clock' times.

Other books to use

Mum can fix it by Verna Allette Wilkins
(Tamarind Books)

The story describes a time when a little girl called Kay, her brother Ben and their mother visit her friend Danny and his family. The story begins at three o'clock when they are about to leave Danny's home, and it tells the time of each event, which is also shown on a clock. The children and their mother face a problem on their way home: the car develops a flat tyre, but Mum is able to fix it and they arrive home just in time – at five o'clock – for Dad's return from work (they have his key).

Provide pictures cut from a spare copy of the book, mix them up and ask the children to put them in the correct order. They could draw pictures to show some of the things which happen in the story; an adult could help to write captions for them.

Ask the children how the story begins: where are the children in the story (at whose home?) and what are they doing? At what time do they have to leave? Why? Talk about what they do when they leave. Ask the children what happens next, and then what happens, and so on.

Grandma's Kitchen
by Liz Graham-Yooll (Ragged Bears)

Something or somebody has been eating things in Grandma's kitchen, beginning at eight o'clock by nibbling the newspaper. A clock shows the time at which each naughty nibble is discovered.

Talk about the times of regular events in the children's day. The children could make up their own stories about mysterious mishaps in any room in the home. Provide clock stamps so that they can show the time at which each event takes place, and help them to make stick-on flaps under which they can show who didn't do it, until the last page of the book, on which they show the real culprit.

The Bad-Tempered Ladybird
by Eric Carle (Picture Puffins)

This is a day in the life of a ladybird. A friendly ladybird flies into the story at sunrise, which is at five o'clock that day, and is soon joined, on a leaf, by a bad-tempered ladybird, which wants to eat all the aphids on the leaf; it offers to fight the friendly ladybird but decides it is too small to bother with. At six o'clock it picks a fight with a larger creature: a wasp. Again the bad-tempered ladybird decides it wants to fight a bigger creature; it meets a stag beetle, but that too is not deemed to be worth fighting, and so off goes the bad-tempered ladybird to find an animal it considers big enough to fight.

And so the story continues: on each hour the ladybird has an aggressive encounter with another creature which it finds too small to fight – until it meets a whale. A clock shows the reader the time of each encounter, and the story ends at six o'clock in the evening.

Have a large clock-face to hand while reading the story to the children; they could help to move the hands to show each time which is mentioned in the story. Ask them which hand stays in the same place for each time. Which one moves? The children could take turns to re-tell the story, using the clock face to show the times.

Did the children notice a time which happened twice in the story (six o'clock)? If necessary, re-read the story after asking them to listen carefully for the time which happens twice. Can they explain why it happens twice? Introduce the words 'morning', 'afternoon', 'evening' and 'night'.

Talk about some of the events of the children's own days. Ask them to think of something which they do in the morning, afternoon, evening and at night. They could draw sequences of four events in a day. Which times happen twice in their days?

Shape and space

Responding to:
How Many Bugs in a Box?
by David A. Carter (Orchard Books)

Intended learning

To develop the children's mathematical language for describing shape, colour, position, and size and their recognition of similar shapes. To encourage the children to notice and describe patterns and to copy them. To develop the ability to recognise, ask and answer questions and to recognise question marks.

The story

The book invites the reader to explore a series of boxes to find out, by lifting flaps and using other cardboard engineering mechanisms, what is inside them.

Each box looks different from the others and one attribute of it is described: for example, its colour, size, shape or pattern. The children learn to recognise and describe shapes, colours and patterns, and they can count the 'bugs' in the boxes.

Key vocabulary

big, blue, curved, green, little, long, on top, narrow, next, red, short, small, straight, tall, thin, underneath, wide

The activity

You will need:

a bag of shopping in which some items are in boxes of different shapes (such as long and short cuboids, large and small cuboids and squares, cylindrical boxes and triangular prisms, long tubes, including more than one of each type); empty cardboard boxes of a variety of different shapes and sizes (there will need to be some which are identical); coloured paper; large gummed paper shapes; wax crayons; felt-tipped pens; painting materials; scissors; glue; sets of objects which will fit inside even the smallest boxes (such as Lego people, or small plastic animals).

Before reading the story

● Talk about boxes: can the children see any boxes in the classroom? What are they used for?

● Ask the children to sort out a bag of shopping according to whether or not the items are in boxes.

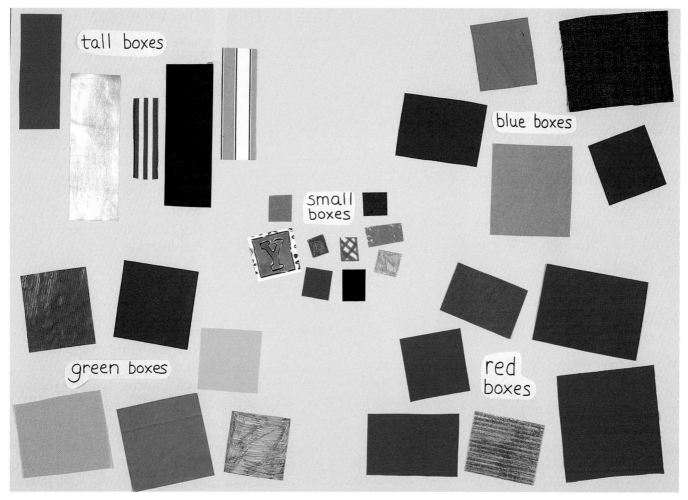

tall boxes

blue boxes

small boxes

green boxes

red boxes

The children cut out one side of a box and decided in which section of the display their own box belonged.

● The children could sort the collection of boxes according to attribute, for example, long, big, small, cylindrical. Can they think of other things which are packaged in boxes of each type?

After reading the story

● Ask the children to look at each box in the book and to describe its size, colour, shape and pattern and anything else they notice. Do they remember what is inside it? They could ask one another questions about the contents of the box and then check to see if the right answers were given.

● Ask the children to choose an empty box which they can decorate by gluing coloured paper on to it, painting or colouring it. If boxes are to be coloured it is best to open them out, turn them inside-out and glue them back together, since the inside usually has a plain, matt, white surface on to which it is easier to apply colour.

● The children could make their own two-dimensional 'lift the flap' box, in which they can draw one or more 'bug' which they can describe. What question will they ask about their boxes? What answer will they give?

Assessment

● Could the children say whether the boxes in the book were big or small/little?

● Could they name their colours?

● Were they able to describe noticeable features of their patterns, such as stripes or spots?

● Could they ask one another questions about the boxes, and could they answer these questions?

● Were the children able to find two or more boxes which were the same shape?

● Could they make a group of boxes which were all 'big' or 'small'?

● Could they find other tall, short, big or small objects?

● Could they find other red, blue or green objects?

Evidence of the children's learning

The children drew, coloured and cut out just one side of a box to look like one of those in the book. An adult helped them to label it, for example, 'a polka dot box', 'a red box', 'a tall box', 'a small box'. They contributed to a display which was sorted into sets of boxes of particular kinds, fixing their boxes to the appropriate section.

Most of the children could find a big or a small box. All of them remembered the unusual boxes, such as 'the polka dot box' and 'the floating box'. Some of them learned the word 'square' and could find square things in the classroom. Some of the children could find examples of tall things such as a lamp-post, a teacher, a cupboard and a door.

Differentiating the activity

To help the children notice what makes one box different from another, ask them to collect boxes which match a description referring to just one attribute, such as: 'a long box', 'a round box', 'a green box'. The children might be able to progress to noticing two attributes: 'a long red box', 'a spotted square box', 'a striped long box'. They could draw boxes which match verbal descriptions given by an adult. Let the children take turns to choose a box which the others can not see: they describe the box, and the others have to find another like it.

Extension activities

The children could look for things in the environment which are big, small, tall, long, short, fat, thin, round and square. They could cut out pictures of such objects and glue them on to a sheet of paper with the appropriate heading.

Provide a collection of pre-cut shapes which are long, short, thin, fat, round and square and ask the children to make patterns in which they can use given numbers of each shape: for example, 'a short shape, two long shapes and a thin shape'. These instructions could be supplied on labelled picture cards.

Play a bingo game using pictures of boxes from the book and from the 'shopping sorting' activity. Each child needs a card on which there are pictures of six different building boxes. The 'caller' needs pictures of the individual boxes.

The 'caller' holds up a picture of a box. If the children have one like it on their cards they cover it with a piece of blank card. The winner is the first to cover all six blocks on his or her card.

Other books to use

Henry's Ball
by Rod Campbell (Campbell Books)

Henry is a dog who has lost his ball. The book shows and describes where he goes to search for the ball, for example; into the garden, along the path, and over the bricks. On the way Henry meets other animals, such as a cat, a snail and a caterpillar, whom he greets and asks whether they have seen his ball.

Finally he goes through a flower bed and asks a bee if it has seen his ball. "It's right under your nose, Henry!" replies the bee, and there it is – hidden by a flap to be lifted by the reader.

Before reading the story, prepare flash cards showing the positional words used in the story: into, along, over, between, beside, under, behind, and through. Show them as they are encountered in the story. Afterwards, ask the children what Henry went into, along, over, between, beside, under, behind, and through. They might need to look at the book to find out.

Copy the words from the book which say where Henry went, such as 'into the garden'. Ask the children to match the words to the pictures.

Using the positional language from the story ask the children to put toy animals into different places. They could draw what they have done, and then choose the flash card which goes with the picture, for example: 'into', 'along', 'over', and so on. They could copy the word from the card.

The Bad-Tempered Ladybird
by Eric Carle (Picture Puffins)

The bad-tempered ladybird is looking for a fight; the first opponent it considers is another ladybird, but that is too small, it says. Swaggering its way through the book, it finds bigger and bigger creatures in its quest for a worthy opponent, until it meets its match – a whale, which dispatches it to the next page with one flick of its tail.

From a spare copy of the book, cut out the pictures of the animals, including the two ladybirds and the aphids. Ask the children to arrange them from smallest to biggest. Write the word 'smallest' at one end of a long piece of paper, such as plain wallpaper or frieze paper; and 'biggest' at the other end. The children could draw the animals the same size as those in the book, and glue them onto the paper in the correct order.

The children could sort the animals by attributes, such as their colour, the number of legs they have, or whether or not they have tails. Some children may be able to sort them using two attributes.

Rosie's Walk
by Pat Hutchins (Picture Puffins)

Rosie the hen goes for a walk one day. Her journey takes her across, around, over, past, through and under things in the farmyard until she is back where she started - at the henhouse.

Make flash cards showing the positional language in the book and, holding up the appropriate card, ask the children what Rosie went around, past, over and so on. They might need to look at the book to find out. They could make up their own story of a walk around the school grounds, saying how different obstacles would need to be traversed, around, over, past, through and under. The 'walks' could be recorded pictorially.

Counting

Responding to:
The Very Hungry Caterpillar
by Eric Carle (Picture Puffins)

Intended learning

To develop the children's understanding of number and knowledge of the days of the week. To develop vocabulary: the names and colours of fruits. For the children to learn to tell events in the order in which they happen.

The story

This is the story of a tiny caterpillar which hatches from an egg on Sunday, eats one apple on Monday, two pears on Tuesday, three plums on Wednesday, four strawberries on Thursday, five oranges on Friday, and an enormous feast on Saturday.

By the Sunday the caterpillar is not very hungry – it has become a very big, fat caterpillar which builds a cocoon around itself, where it stays for two weeks after which it emerges – not as a caterpillar but as a beautiful butterfly.

Key vocabulary

one, two, three, four, five, Sunday, Monday, Tuesday, Wednesday, Thursday, Friday, Saturday, day, week

The activity

You will need:

two apples, four pears, six plums, eight strawberries, ten oranges; coloured paper, scissors and glue; paint and sponges for printing, art paper, photographs of fruits.

Before reading the story

● Talk about caterpillars the children have seen; ask them about their size and colour, and anything else they noticed about them. If possible, show the children a plant or leaf which has been partially eaten by caterpillars.

● What do caterpillars eat? How can we tell?

● Do the children know what caterpillars grow into?

● Show the children the cover of the book and ask them how many heads, eyes, noses, feelers and feet the caterpillar has. Count aloud the caterpillar's segments, encouraging the children to join in as far as they can.

After reading the story

● Talk about the day the caterpillar hatched from its egg: can the children remember what day it was? Practise reciting the days of the week - do the children know which day comes after Sunday?

● Provide the children with A5 cards on each of which has been written a numeral from 1-5, a word for one of these numerals and a quantity of fruits from 1-5. Ask them to make matching sets. The children could draw one of their matching sets.

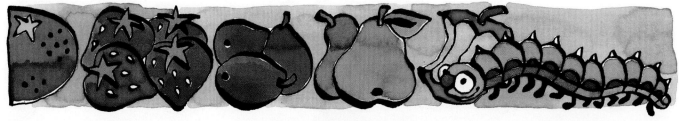

● Ask the children whether the caterpillar eats more or fewer fruits each day. How many more? Help the children to count in twos from 2 to 10. They could arrange in rows which increase in two, and then draw, everyday classroom objects. The drawing will be a simple pictogram.

● Provide a set of real fruits, the same as those in the story, and ask the children to look carefully at any of the fruits; draw attention to their shape and colour. Ask the children to paint a large picture of that group of fruits.

Help them to write a caption to accompany it, for example: 'On Monday the caterpillar ate through one apple'.

● When their paintings are dry, cut out the fruits, help them to punch a hole through each of them to show where the caterpillar ate it, and mount a selection of them, with their captions, on the caterpillar display.

Each of the segments of our caterpillar could be lifted up to display the children's captioned paintings underneath.

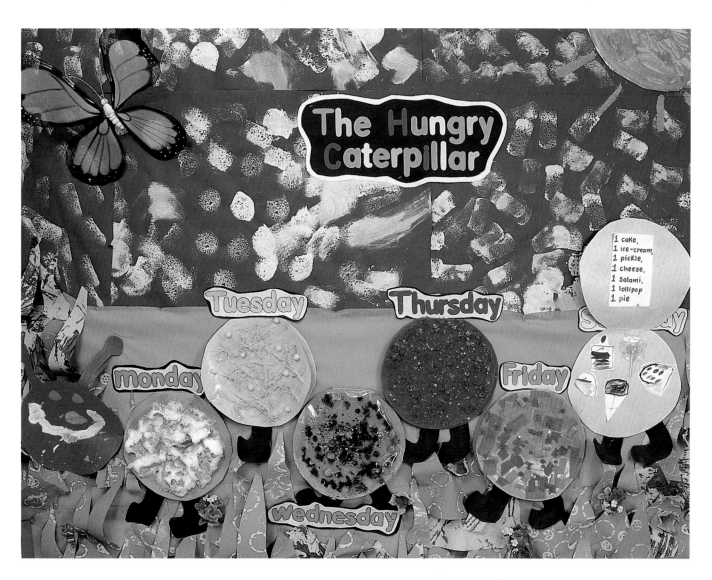

Assessment

● Can the children count the fruits eaten by the caterpillar each day? (Up to what number can they count?)

● Do they know the names of some of the days of the week?

● Are they able to match quantities of one to five with the appropriate numerals? (Up to what number can they do this?)

● Can they match the words to the appropriate numerals? (Up to what number can they do this?)

● Can the children identify and name familiar fruits?

Evidence of the children's learning

The children could answer the question 'How many eggs are on the leaf?' They knew that only one caterpillar hatched out (some of them remembered but others had to check by looking at the picture). They found out from the book how many apples the caterpillar ate through on Monday, what it ate on Tuesday and how many, and so on. With help, the children counted the foods through which the caterpillar ate each day. Some of the children could recognise the names of the days of the week on a calendar.

Each child printed one segment of an enormous caterpillar to form part of a display. They printed on it patches of different shades of green; when each piece was dry they cut it into the shape of a segment of the caterpillar. We counted with them the total number of segments made by their groups. The segments made by all groups of children were assembled to make the body of a caterpillar, and some children made the head. When it was finished, we counted all the segments with the children.

Differentiating the activity

For children who do not know the names of the fruits, or who have difficulty with counting, make a display of the same fruits as those in the story (one apple, two pears, three plums, four strawberries and five oranges) and ask them to make the right number of flour-and-water dough models of each fruit. Help them to make a hole through each fruit to show the part which has been eaten by the caterpillar.

When their models are dry help them to mix the right colours with which to paint them. Ask them to name their fruits and help them to count them.

The children could demonstrate their model fruits while re-telling the story.

Extension activities

Provide the children with photographs of groups of fruits (the same fruits but not necessarily the same numbers as in the story) and ask them to count them. They could sort them into sets which are 'right' and 'wrong', according to the numbers the caterpillar ate, for example a card showing one apple is 'right', but one showing two apples is 'wrong'.

Involving parents

Ask parents to count fruits with the children when they buy them or when they take them out of the shopping bag. The children could draw all the fruit they eat in a day; ask parents to help them write captions for their drawings, for example: 'On Monday I ate one apple and five grapes.'

Other books to use

One Bear at Bedtime
by Mick Inkpen (Hodder)

A little boy daydreams while he thinks about his teddy bear at bedtime. He imagines two pigs who wear his clothes, three kangaroos who bounce on his bed, four giraffes who sit in the bath, and so on, up to a monster with ten heads who takes for ever to say goodnight.

With the children, count the creatures (or heads, in the case of the monster) on each page. They could make up their own 'One Bear at Bedtime' stories which continue up to numbers with which they can cope; ask them to draw different creatures from those in the story and help them to write the appropriate number on each picture.

Ten Little Crocodiles
by Colin West (Walker Books)

This rhyming story opens with ten little crocodiles sitting down to dine; the rhyming outcome of this is 'One ate too much pud and then there were nine!' The rhyme continues with the number of crocodiles diminishing as they exercise in a gym, pray, do magic tricks, learn to drive, go sailing, go skiing, visit the zoo and sit in the sun, until only one sad little crocodile, who misses all his friends, remains.

Invite the children to join in the reading of the story, completing the missing word (the number of crocodiles left) at the end of each double-page spread. If they are not yet able to subtract one from numbers up to ten, the rhyme will help them: dine/nine, weight/eight, heaven/seven, tricks/six, drive/five, shore/four, ski/three, zoo/two and sun/one.

Rooster's off to See the World
by Eric Carle (Puffin)

Rooster decides to leave home to see the world. As he sets off he encounters groups of animals whom he invites to join him, beginning with two cats, then three frogs, and so on up to five fish. Each new group is clearly drawn so that the children can count, and is also drawn in black and white outline to form a block graph on the same page.

After the fish join the adventure the animals realise that Rooster has not organised it very well ('Where's our dinner?' ask the cats, and 'Where are we supposed to sleep?' ask the frogs). Gradually each group of animals leaves, in reverse order to that in which they joined Rooster: first the five fish, then the four turtles, and so on, until rooster is alone again.

Ask the children to count the animals in each group, for example, 'How many roosters are there?', 'How many cats are there?'. Some children might be able to count the whole collection of animals as each group joins it or leaves it.

A world of science

Responding to:
Who Sank the Boat?
by Pamela Allen (Picture Puffins)

Intended learning

To encourage the children to try to make sense of their observations of the world around them and to develop their understanding of the ways in which objects behave in water. To develop the ability to retell stories.

The story

A cow, a donkey, a sheep, a pig and a mouse are good friends who, for no particular reason, decide to go out in a rowing boat. One by one they get into the small rowing boat, tipping it and rocking it, but somehow managing to squeeze in and balance it – until the tiny mouse jumps on board, whereupon the boat sinks.

Key vocabulary

balanced, heavy, heaviest, level, light, lightest, sank, tilted, weight

The activity

You will need:

a collection of toy boats and sets of model animals which will fit into them (including a cow, a donkey, a sheep, a pig and a mouse); a water tray or bowl of water in which to float the boats; a transparent plastic aquarium tank; recycled materials.

Before reading the story

● Talk about things which float: can the children name some things which float and some which sink?

● Provide a collection of objects (such as three plastic bottles (one empty, one filled with water and one filled with sand); a foil tray; a ball; a wooden block; an empty photographic film container; a similar film container full of sand; a stone; and a sponge) for the children to put into a plastic aquarium tank (a transparent container is useful because it allows the children to see which objects sink right to the bottom of the water, which ones float and which ones sink beneath the surface of the water but not to the bottom).

● Help the children to record their results by drawing and labelling the objects and placing them in the appropriate place on a drawing of the water tray or tank which shows a side view.

● Ask the children about boats they have seen: rowing boats, liners, rafts, canoes, and so on. Show them pictures of a range of boats and ask them which could hold the heaviest load or the greatest number of people without sinking. Can they think of anything that might sink a boat?

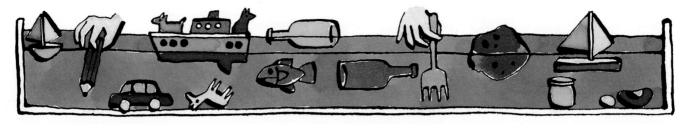

We filled transparent bottles with water and sand (and left the other bottle empty but with the lid on). The children took turns to experiment with each of the bottles, observing how each behaved when dropped into a tank of water.

After reading the story

● Talk about the effect which each animal had when it got into the boat. Record the children's responses during the discussion.

● Talk about the meaning of 'balance': to show its meaning, ask the children to balance the ends of a see-saw, and then a weighing balance.

● The children could play with a small collection of toy boats in a water tray (provide a water tray and a collection of toy boats which includes a range of shapes and sizes, some of which might be non-floating model boats, and a collection of model animals).

● Ask them which boats they think will hold the set of model animals; let them find out. What happens when they put all the animals at one end or to one side of the boat? What difference does it make when they balance them? They could draw pictures to show the best way to arrange the animals in the boat.

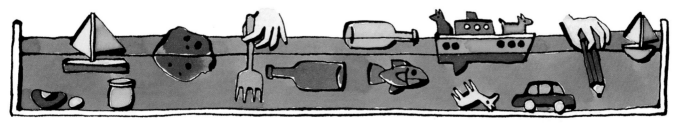

Assessment

● Can the children say why the boat tipped up when the cow and pig got into it but not when the donkey and sheep climbed aboard?

● Do the children realise that the tiny mouse could sink the boat because the boat already had in it as much weight as it could take?

● When putting model animals in a toy boat, do the children arrange them so that they balance the boat?

● Do the children place their drawings to record floating and sinking objects in appropriate places on the picture of the aquarium tank?

● Do the model boats which the children make show that they understand the need for a hollow shape?

● Can the children retell the story (or some of it) while looking at the pictures in the book and re-creating it using model animals?

Evidence of the children's learning

Some of the children realised that if the cow had stepped into the middle of the boat it might not have tipped one end of it. They noticed that the boat did not tip when the donkey got in: 'it balanced'.

Some of them could explain what happened when the pig got into the boat, and why: 'it tipped because the pig sat on the side.' We looked at the pictures to decide why the boat didn't tip up when the sheep got in (it sat in a place where it balanced the pig's weight).

A few children could say how the tiny mouse sank the boat: 'The boat was full up, so even the tiny mouse was too heavy.'

Differentiating the activity

To help children to retell the story, provide toy boats and a set of model animals for them to use as props as they look at the pictures in the book; encourage them to talk about what is happening in the pictures. Afterwards, they could draw pictures to record the story.

Extension activities

The children could make model boats; allow them to choose the materials from a collection which includes items such as hollowed-out halves of grapefruits, melons, coconuts or oranges, cocktail sticks, card, foil dishes, plastic food trays and small boxes.

How will they make sure their boat will float? Will it hold the set of toy animals without sinking?

The children could test their model boats and draw pictures to show them in the water with the set of model animals in them.

The children could find different ways to sink a floating plastic food tray: they could fill it with water; put something in one corner of it to unbalance it; make a hole in it; or put a heavy weight in it. Let them draw, then test, their ideas. You could display them under the heading 'How to sink a boat'.

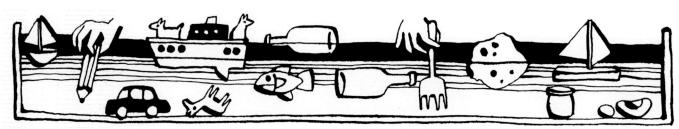

Other books to use for science:

LIFE CYCLES OF PLANTS:

Jack and the Beanstalk
(Traditional, Ladybird Read-it-Yourself series)

Jack's mother sends him to market to sell their cow because they can no longer afford to keep it. On the way Jack meets a man who gives him some magic beans in exchange for the cow. Jack's mother is furious; she throws the beans into the garden, where they grow into a huge beanstalk. Despite his mother's dire warnings, Jack climbs the beanstalk. At the top he finds the home of a giant. While the giant sleeps Jack makes off with a bag of money, which the giant had stolen from Jack's father. During subsequent raids Jack retrieves more stolen goods: his late father's hen and magic harp. But on the last raid the giant spots Jack and chases him down the beanstalk; in the nick of time Jack reaches the bottom, calls for his mother to bring an axe, and chops down the beanstalk, killing the giant in his fall.

Show the children a collection of beans, including haricots, chilli beans, mung beans, black-eyed beans and broad beans, and ask the children to look closely for ways in which the beans are similar and how they are different; warn them not to put them in their mouths (close supervision is needed). They should notice that all have a place from which a shoot will grow (the hilum), but that they are of different sizes and different colours. Which do they think will grow into the tallest beanstalk?

Help them to plant their beans in small pots of potting compost. To record the type of bean planted, seal a sample bean in a small piece of polythene and fix it to the side of the pot using Sellotape. Compare the growth of the beans at intervals of three or four days. Some beans could be planted in clear plastic containers, between the side of the container and a piece of damp kitchen paper, to allow the children to see when they first sprout.

LIFE CYCLES OF ANIMALS:

The Very Hungry Caterpillar
by Eric Carle (Picture Puffins)

This is the story of a tiny caterpillar which hatches from an egg and spends a week sleeping, and eating its way through increasing amounts of food each day for a week, culminating with a virtual banquet. After this, not surprisingly, the caterpillar is not very hungry – it has become a very big, fat caterpillar which builds a cocoon around itself, where it stays for two weeks, after which it emerges – not as a caterpillar but as a beautiful butterfly.

Talk about the stages in the caterpillar's life: the children could make a collage which depicts the life of the caterpillar, ending with a beautiful butterfly, for which they could use a range of brightly coloured papers and fabrics, including foil and cellophane, felt and brocade. The collage could be presented as a simple time line which shows the length, in weeks, of each stage of the caterpillar's life.

Do the children know other animals which change their whole form as they grow? Examples include: birds, frogs and toads. They could find pictures of them in reference books.

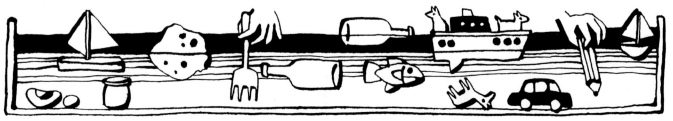

Where I live

Responding to:
Cat among the cabbages
by Alison Bartlett (Levinson Books)

Intended learning

For the children to recognise and learn the names of the features of the area in which they live and of specific environments: a garden and farm yard. To introduce the idea that an environment can be recorded as a pictorial map and for the children to be able to trace a journey on a pictorial map.

To develop the ability to recognise frequently-used words in a story and in the environment, and vocabulary for sizes, colours, sounds and movements.

The story

A big white cat is asleep in the sun. After stretching and yawning, he sets off for a walk, seemingly looking for something. He walks through some blue paint and so his pawprints are easy to follow. We hear what the cat sees and what he does on his walk and there are descriptions of the sizes and colours of the things he passes, and of the sounds they and the cat make.

Key vocabulary

barn, big, black, blue, brown, enormous, fat, field, gate, green, high, huge, large, little, long, low, medium-sized, path, pink, red, small, tiny, white, yellow

The activity

You will need:

painting materials; sponges for printing paw-prints; felt-tipped pens; wax crayons; scissors; glue; paper; fabric scraps; recycled materials such as cardboard boxes, pieces of smooth wood, lollipop sticks, paper, plastic and silk flowers, dried flowers, grass and straw, pages from magazines, cardboard tubes, matting, foil, silver paper, sweet wrappers and wood shavings; two spare copies of the book from which the pictures of the places through which the cat goes have been cut, glued on to card and laminated on both sides; *Blu-tac*.

Before reading the story

● Talk about the children's own experiences of journeys, if any: where did the journey start, where did it end, what did they pass on the way?

● Do the children come to school or nursery on foot, on a bus, in a car, or in another way? They could talk about the people with whom they travel and what they pass on the way: for example, shops (which shops?), roads (what are their names?), trees, grass, footpaths, houses (what are they like?) and gardens (what is in them?).

● How do the children know when they are getting near the school, even before they can see it? Talk about 'landmarks' or 'things to look out for'.

● Do the children know the names of any of the roads they crossed or travelled along on their way to school? They could think of other words for roads, such as avenue, place, square, close, view, street and so on. Display the names of local roads as they appear on their signs.

We made a display of the cat's journey past the different landmarks.

After reading the story

● Once the children have enjoyed the initial reading of the story, re-read it, asking them to identify, from a collection of everyday classroom objects and materials, things to show where the cat was at each stage of his walk (they should look carefully at the illustrations to help them choose the most suitable materials). They could, for example, choose a piece of green fabric or matting to show where the cat is at the start of the story (on a lawn), and then find something to represent the big blue gate, the tangled leaves and tiny pea-pods, the neat rows of huge cabbages and the field of little yellow flowers.

● Once they have completed this three-dimensional pictorial map of the journey, the children could paint or make collages of the 'landmarks' they have identified. Help them to arrange these in the correct order on a display board and use different-sized sponges to print the cat's blue pawprints on to the display.

● Talk about the way in which the cat moves; the children could each paint and cut out a picture of a big white cat, performing one of the activities described in the story. Ask them to find, on the pictorial map display, where the cat does this: for example, he crouches, then leaps in the field of flowers; he struts past small pink piglets by the white fence. Label the pictures with the words for the cat's actions.

● Take the children for a short walk around the school or nursery grounds or the local environment and encourage them to notice where they started and what they pass during the walk. If possible, take photographs of the places and objects passed during the walk. Back in the classroom, ask them to describe each stage of the journey. They could draw each of these stages and an adult could help to label them. Their labelled drawings could be put in order and displayed with photographs to make a pictorial map of the walk.

Assessment

● Can the children identify, on the pictorial map which they have helped to make, some of the places through which the cat in the story goes and some of the things and animals it sees?

● Can they identify, on the pictorial map, where the cat does each of its activities?

● Can they distinguish between the path, the grass and the fields on the pictorial map of the story?

● Are the children able to describe a local journey, talking about some of the landmarks passed?

● Can they arrange, in the correct order, things to represent landmarks on their own walks?

● Can they describe a lane, street, hill, road or avenue they know?

● How well do the children recognise familiar words such as 'Stop', 'Bus stop', 'Street', 'Road' and 'Avenue'.

Evidence of the children's learning

The children could remember some landmarks they pass: 'We go past the sweet shop', 'I see the park on my way to nursery', 'a lollipop lady helps us to cross the road'. One child said that her street had big houses at one end and little houses at the other. Another said that only one car at a time could go down his road.

On their map of the cat's walk, the children used drinking straws painted blue to make the gate. They used a mixture of materials to represent leaves, mixing these with a sprig of real leaves.

Differentiating the activity

Children who have difficulty in recognising the sequence of the story could retell the story using the book as a prompt; then they could do the same using the pictorial map which the whole class has made to show the cat's journey. As they come to each part of the cat's journey, ask them to find it in the story book.

Extension activities

Make a game, by cutting out and laminating illustrations from a spare copy of the book and giving one each to a small group of children (make a separate pile for the pictures which are left over). Ask the children to follow the cat's journey on the big pictorial map they have made as you read the story.

They have to say 'stop' when the reader comes to a place of which they have a picture. Using Blu-tac, fix their picture alongside its counterpart on the map, take another picture from the pile and take a counter. If they fail to stop the reader, they cannot put their picture on the map or take a counter, but another child may do it for them and earn the counter. The winner is the child with the most counters at the end of the story.

Involving parents

Encourage parents to talk to the children about their routes between home and school; they could point out 'landmarks' such as shops or other buildings, noticeable trees, gardens, zebra crossings, traffic lights and post boxes. They could help the children to look for a landmark which tells them that they are nearly at school (before they can see the school itself) and the same for their homes on the way back from school.

Other books to use

Each Peach Pear Plum
by Janet and Allan Ahlberg (Picture Puffins)

The title page of this book features an oblique aerial-view illustration of the landscape in which the action takes place. Each double-page spread features an 'I spy' rhyme on one page, with an illustration on the opposite page, in which the reader has to find the characters (they are all nursery rhyme characters), and each double page spread leads on to the next, for example:

'Each Peach Pear Plum
I spy Tom Thumb'

(Tom Thumb is hiding in a tree in the illustration.)

'Tom Thumb in the cupboard
I spy Mother Hubbard'

Make a large coloured drawing or painting (a copy of the oblique aerial-view picture) and, after reading each rhyme, ask the children where, on this picture, the character might be; they should explain their answers. Point out some 'wrong' places and ask 'Why couldn't he/she/they be here?'; ask them also if they could be anywhere else.

Help the children to continue the rhyming story, adding more characters and choosing places on the picture where they might be found.

The large copy of the picture could form the background for a display on to which the children glue their cut-out drawings of characters in the book, such as Tom Thumb, Mother Hubbard, the Three Bears and Baby Bunting.

The Train Ride
by June Crebbin (Walker Books)

The story describes all the things a little girl sees through the windows of a train as she goes with her mother to visit her grandma: sheep on a hillside and cows in a meadow, a mare and a foal on a hill, a tractor in a field, a tunnel, geese by a pond, a hot air balloon in the sky, a bridge, a viaduct, a market square, a seaside village, a harbour, a lighthouse, the sea and beach, and a station. Some of these are named but others are just shown in the illustrations.

Help the children to make a frieze of the journey which shows the landscape and anything in it: features such as a bridge, tunnel or viaduct. Along the frieze should be a railway track. The train could be drawn, painted and cut out, then attached to the frieze. Along the frieze write some of the words of the story.

The children could retell the story using a model train and passengers, having first created the landscape alongside the track using construction kits and recycled materials.

The past

Responding to:
Once There Were Giants
by Martin Waddell (Walker Books)

Intended learning

To develop the children's understanding of chronology in terms of the important and memorable events in their own lives and in those of other people; and for them to discover the similarities and differences between the care of babies in their own and their parents' generations.

For the children to use their experiences of stories as a basis for their own story-telling and/or writing.

The story

This is the story of a lifetime. Mum and Dad and big brother and sister were giants – to the baby whose life story is told up to the time when she, too, is a giant. It describes milestones in her life such as when she could first sit up and was given a high chair, when she first sat at the table with the rest of her family, learning to crawl, walk, talk and run, going to playschool, then to infant, junior and senior school, followed by her first job, her wedding and the birth of her own little girl – to whom she was a giant.

Against the backdrop of childhood games, memorable events and achievements we read about the times when she was naughty, and the things which worried, frightened and delighted her. It is presented as a series of delightful illustrations which are almost snapshots from a family album, with captions.

Key vocabulary

baby, crawl, cry, Dad, giant, Mum, play, run, school, sit, small, talk, walk, work

The activity

You will need:

two copies of the book; photographs of each of the children, and their families from birth up to the present; scissors; glue; clear adhesive covering; paper; felt-tip pens, clothes' catalogues.

Before reading the story

● Talk about the children's memories from when they were younger, even when they were babies. What events do they remember? They might remember achievements such as learning a new skill like skipping, hopping or whistling; happy events such as days out or holidays, sad events such as a death, getting lost or losing or breaking a favourite toy, or milestones such as birthdays.

● Ask the children about things which made them happy, sad or worried.

● Using long strips of card, the children could make time-lines of their own lives so far, showing their birthdays and two or three 'big events' which they remember. They could find out, from their parents, at what ages they learned to sit up, crawl, talk and walk. Pictures to show these events could be added to their time-lines.

We cut pictures out of clothing catalogues showing people at different ages and asked the children to put them in age order.

After reading the story

● Ask the children who were the giants at the beginning of the story. Who thought they were giants and why? Talk about the giants in their own families. What do they remember doing with their own giants?

● Can they find the picture and text in the story which show the little girl at their own age? How can they tell she is their age?

● Ask the children to look for the time in the story when the little girl herself becomes a giant. They might think it is the last page, where she says she is one of the giants, or they may choose a time at which she first looks grown up.

● Ask the children to compare the pictures on pages 7 and 29 of the book (in which the central character is a baby and a mother, respectively). What can they find in each picture which is the same? What differences can they find? Draw the children's attention to the soft toys; the greetings cards on both mantelpieces (ask what the cards might be for); the nappy-changing paraphernalia; people are looking at the baby and helping to look after her; some of the same people are in both pictures (note how they have changed).

Assessment

● Can the children talk about events in their own past?

● Can they identify 'giants' in their own families, and talk about things they have done with them?

● Can they find the time in the story when the little girl was their own age, and say how they can tell?

● Are the children able to put in order a set of pictures from the story, and to explain how they know the order?

● Can they put in order a series of photographs from their own lives, and talk to a partner about each picture?

● Can the children identify some of the similarities and differences between the first and last pictures of the story?

● Can the children sort a set of clothes into 'clothes for a baby/clothes for us'? Are they able to identify differences and similarities between pictures of themselves and of their parents as babies?

Evidence of the children's learning

We asked a group of children to put in order a set of pictures cut from magazines showing different stages in the life of a human being from birth to old age; when they had done so we gave them an extra picture and asked them to decide where it should go in the sequence. The children then used this sequence of pictures to help them retell the story of how people change as they grow.

Differentiating the activity

For children who have difficulty with the concept of chronology, provide an assorted collection of baby clothes and clothes suitable for the children in the class and ask them to sort them: clothes for a baby/clothes for us; label and display the two sets of clothes. How can the children tell which clothes are for a baby and which are for themselves?

The children could look for baby clothes and clothes for themselves in catalogues; help them to cut them out and glue them onto two pages, headed 'Clothes for a baby' and 'Clothes for me'.

Extension activities

With a partner each child could put in order a series of photographs from his or her own life, then tell the partner about each picture: what is happening, who the people are, and ending in the same way as each page of the story: 'The one [description of what he or she is doing] is me.'

The children could look at pictures of babies of their own and their parents' generations. What differences and similarities can they identify? Point out such things as clothes, toys, baby equipment such as seats, prams and pushchairs.

Involving parents

Encourage parents to show the children and talk to them about family photographs and any records they have kept of the children's growth and learning when they were babies, for example: the ages at which they first sat up, crawled, walked, talked and ran. They could talk about other people in the photographs, what everyone was doing and anything memorable which happened. The children could show some of these photographs and memorabilia to the class and talk about them.

Other books to use

Mr Wolf's Week
by Colin Hawkins (Mammoth)

The story starts on Monday. It is wet, so Mr Wolf puts on his raincoat and rubber boots, carries his umbrella and strides out into the rain. The children can follow the picture sequence which shows what happens to him. Then Tuesday comes. It is foggy, so Mr Wolf wears his checked coat, yellow scarf and red cap. This time the picture story has speech bubbles. The story continues throughout the week; each day the weather is described and the reader is told what Mr Wolf wears and takes out with him before braving the weather, and each time there is a picture sequence to show what happens to him. The story ends on Sunday, and then the week begins again.

Talk about the children's week. Can they remember what the weather was like each day, and what they wore? They could begin a diary for each day of the week which describes the weather and what they wore. They might be able to tell or write a story about what happened during the day.

Provide calendars, diaries and other printed material which shows the days of the week, and show the children where to find the date.

Make 'days of the week' flash cards. Each day the children could take turns to say what day it is and to find the right card to display.

The Baby
by John Burningham (Red Fox)

The story describes a new baby: how he eats, what he can and cannot do and what his mother, father and older brother do to look after him. It shows bath-time, feeding time and nappy-changing time. The little boy in the story likes the baby some of the time, but not always (when he cries). The book ends by saying that the baby can not yet play with his big brother, who hopes he will grow up soon.

Talk about the things that babies can and cannot do. What do people need to do for them? The children could describe how they have changed since they were babies. What can they do now which they could not do then?

Help the children to make a booklet which could be called 'Babies can't but we can', in which they can glue pictures of babies, under which an adult has written, after discussion with the children, their ideas, for example: 'The baby can't use a spoon but I can', 'The baby can't make a sandcastle but I can'.

From Snowflakes to Sandcastles
by Annie Owen (Frances Lincoln)

This is the story of a child's year, from snowflakes in January, to August with days on the beach, and on to December with Christmas trees and presents. Each month of the year has a double page spread: one with headlines, such as, for January: 'snow-balls, gloves, torches, snowflakes, mittens, boots, slippers, scarves, woolly hats, snowmen, hot-water bottles, snowdrops, moon'. Then the reader is asked to find in a busy illustration such things as 'two spotty mittens', and 'the blue slippers'. They are asked questions such as: 'Which glove is the odd one out?' and 'Where are the blue slippers?'

Provide a collection of calendars with illustrations or photographs, take them apart and help the children to put the months in order. Do they know the months or time of the year in which the following happen: their birthday, Christmas (or Divali, Ramadan or other familiar celebration), summer holidays, conkers fall from horse chestnut trees, and so on?

Ask the children to think of things to draw for the current month, for example the flowers and trees in bloom; the birds they notice (particularly notable seasonal visitors); stages of animal life cycles (caterpillars, tadpoles and so on); the things they do, wear and eat; and celebrations they see, about which they learn or in which they take part.

What I can do

Responding to:
We're Going on a Bear Hunt
by Michael Rosen (Walker Books)

Intended learning

To develop the children's awareness of space and their ability to control their movements as they move under, over and through large apparatus.

For the children to remember a story they have heard and to develop the skill of re-enacting it.

The story

A family goes for a walk: parents, a little boy, a little girl, a baby and a dog. The story describes their actions as they traverse tall grass, a river, thick oozy mud, a dark forest, a swirling snow-storm, until they reach a narrow gloomy cave, in which they discover a bear.

They retrace their steps, rush into their home, close the door just in time to keep out the bear, and dive under the bedclothes.

Key vocabulary

down, into, over, splash, squelch, stumble, swish, through, tiptoe, trip, under, up

The activity

You will need:

a collection of large apparatus which the children can move over, under and through, representing the journey of the family in the story; pictures of people moving across or through sand, thick mud, ice, snow, and water.

Before reading the story

● Talk about the ways in which the children can move across different materials.

● How can they move across a hard floor? Let them try their ideas.

● How might they move across a soft floor?

● What difference does the floor make? How can they move across a sand pit, a grassy hill, a big rock, or a pile of cushions?

● On what kind of surface is it difficult to walk? The children could think about walking through water up to their waists, thick mud, bushes and across ice or snow.

● They could look at reference books to find out how people cross difficult surfaces and talk about the ways in which they could make this easier: for example, wearing snow-shoes or ice skates, or using a boat.

● Do the children know the words for different ways to move? Show them pictures of people wading, swimming, floating, skating, tramping, shuffling, hopping and skipping and invite them to find the picture which matches a word called out.

After reading the story

● Talk about the way in which the people in the book moved through the long grass; lifting their feet high, pushing them through the grass and parting the grass with their hands and arms (demonstrate this and encourage the children to join in). Show them the picture of the family in the book wading through the river, and ask them what they were doing with their arms, whether it would be easy to walk through a river, and why not.

● Show the children the picture of the people walking through the mud, and ask them what they were doing with their feet, why they could not walk properly, whether they themselves had ever walked through thick mud and what it felt like.

● Talk about going through the dark forest, and why the people stumbled and tripped. Show the children the picture of the family struggling through the snowstorm, ask them if they have ever been out in a snowstorm or a strong wind, what it was like, and what made it hard to walk.

● Ask the children to pretend they are walking through grass which is up to their waists, moving their legs as if they have to push their way through long grass, and parting it with their arms. They could repeat the words from the story as they do so: 'Swishy swashy, swishy swashy'.

● Similarly the children could pretend they are crossing the other obstacles met by the family in the story, moving in the way the characters in the story moved, and repeating the words from the book as they do so: the river ('Splash, splosh, splash, splosh'), the mud ('Squelch squerch, squelch squerch'), the dark forest ('Stumble, trip, stumble, trip'), the snow-storm ('Hoooo, woooo, hoooo, woooo') and the cave ('Tiptoe, tiptoe, tiptoe, tiptoe').

We were able to make use of the long grass in the school's wildflower garden to recreate the journey of the characters in the story. The children pushed their way through the grass saying 'swishy swashy, swishy swashy' as they did so.

Assessment

● Can the children distinguish between the kinds of movements people make as they cross different obstacles?

● Can they identify what someone is pretending to cross?

● Do they make appropriate movements as they pretend to cross long grass, mud, and so on?

● Observe the quality of the children's movements, for example: when crossing 'long grass' do they lift their feet high and push against the imaginary grass; when crossing 'mud' do they pretend their feet are difficult to lift?

● Observe the children playing on the 'bear hunt' course: how much of the available space do they use? How do they move their arms and legs? How confident are their movements? How well do they control their movements?

● How well can the children re-enact the story? (Note the number of obstacles they remember and the words from the story which they use.)

Evidence of the children's learning

The children helped to set up the journey of the characters in the book, using large apparatus, such as climbing frames, benches, mats, and large blocks. We were able to make use of the long grass in the school grounds; the children used blue mats to make the river, torn paper to make the snowstorm and part of a climbing frame, covered with strips of plastic cut from bin bags to make the cave. They put a teddy bear in the cave. They took turns to retrace the journey of the characters in the story.

Differentiating the activities

For children who have difficulty in understanding what types of movements and/or sounds are indicated by the different words such as 'stumble', 'swish' and 'splosh', an adult helper could demonstrate the ways in which the family in the book moved when crossing the different obstacles they encountered; provide a copy of the book and ask the children where you are: in the river? in the snowstorm? and so on. How can they tell? Ask them to try the movements themselves. Gradually they could choose and demonstrate movements from the story for the rest of the group to identify.

Extension activities

The children could make up their own 'journey' stories, in which they have to face obstacles, such as: a strong wind, cobblestones, rocks, a mountain, or tangled bushes and creepers. Ask them to act these stories in groups and help them to recreate the places in which they happen. Talk about the ways in which they move their bodies as they cross different kinds of obstacles. Record and display their responses.

Involving parents

At home or out and about, parents could talk to their children about different ways of moving. They could talk about the ways in which they move across cobbles, gravel, grass, mud and tarmac. They could play 'follow my leader': the leader not only performs the actions, but describes them: for example, 'hop-hop', 'little jump, little jump', 'big stride, big stride'.

Provide notebooks in which parents can record the words they have used with their children. Read them with the children and ask them to repeat the words and perform the corresponding actions for the rest of the group or class.

Other books to use

I'm Going on a Dragon Hunt
by Maurice Jones (Puffin)

In this story a little boy sets off to hunt dragons. He encounters similar obstacles to those met by the family in We're Going on a Bear Hunt: *long grass, a river, a tall tree, a deep ravine, and thick mud, but he finds different ways to cross them.*

Before reading the story, ask the children what they might do if they came to long grass, a wide river, and so on. After reading the story they could pretend to cross the obstacles encountered. As they do so they could talk, with help, about the ways in which they are moving, for example: "I can't swim under it, stretching my arms and flapping my feet", "I'll have to sail across it, tugging the sail of my boat as the wind blows it."

Set up a 'dragon hunt' area in which the children can play or recreate the story.

Buster's Day
by Rod Campbell (Campbell Books)

Buster finds plenty to do from the moment he wakes until he goes to bed: he helps with the washing, gives his kitten a saucer of milk, plays in the kitchen, has something to eat, goes into the garden, looks over the fence, watches the birds, plays with the hosepipe, has a bath – then goes to bed.

Talk about Buster's day and encourage the children to act some of the things he does; can the others guess what they are doing? (They could look at the book if necessary). Provide a role-play area which has a 'kitchen', 'garden' and 'bedroom', in which the children can play and act the story of Buster's day.

Cat among the cabbages
by Alison Bartlett (Levinson Books)

The big white cat moves in many different ways during his walk around the garden and into the farmyard: he stretches, walks, steps, crouches, leaps, struts, runs and creeps, until he stops at the barn. There he finds what he has been looking for: the medium-sized black cat and lots of small black and white kittens.

After the children have enjoyed the first reading of the story, read it again, asking them to move in the way the cat moves: how is strutting different from walking? Can they show how creeping and stepping are different from walking?

The children could take turns to perform the actions of the cat in the story for the others, who have to say which action it is.

Introduce other words for different ways of walking: for example, stride, stroll, rush and clomp. Talk about their meanings and ask the children to walk in the way described.

Little Bird
by Rod Campbell (Campbell Books)

Little Bird is sad because she cannot do the things which the other animals can, such as roaring and growling, swinging from the trees and lifting heavy things. The other animals show off what they can do. Then Little Bird realises that there is something very special she can do, and so she is happy.

After the children have enjoyed the story, ask them which animals can swing through trees, slide through grass, jump over a log, and so on. Provide apparatus and mats over, under and along which the children can perform an animal's action when you call its name: for example, 'snake' (slide through grass).

Patterns and colours

Responding to:
Elmer by David McKee (Red Fox)

Intended learning

For the children to explore colour and pattern in two-dimensional work and to talk about pictures and patterns which they see and which they themselves create.

To develop the children's ability to recognise critical features of words such as shape, ascenders and descenders.

The story

Elmer is different from all the other elephants – he is not elephant-coloured, but a yellow, orange, red, pink, purple, blue, green, black and white PATCHWORK! He is the happiest and funniest elephant in the herd. One day he decides that he wants to look like the other elephants. He finds a bush on which grow elephant-coloured berries which he crushes to make a juice. He covers himself with the juice until he looks just like the other elephants. He rejoins the herd and is not recognised.

After a while he wonders what is different about the herd; then he realises that not one of them is smiling. He has to do something about this, so he shouts 'Boo!' and then rolls on his back laughing. 'It must be Elmer!' say the other elephants, just as it begins to rain, washing off Elmer's new colour. All the elephants agree that this is Elmer's funniest joke ever and plan to celebrate it on that date every year, by decorating themselves in brightly coloured patterns, while Elmer covers himself with the elephant-coloured juice.

Key vocabulary

black, blue, green, grey, multi-coloured, orange, patchwork, pink, purple, red, white, yellow

The activity

You will need:

reference books and pictures of elephants, painting materials, white art paper, sugar paper, glue, scissors, coloured paper, paper of different colours from magazines and brochures, used gift-wrapping paper, wallpaper, felt-tips of different thicknesses, and a card on which the word 'elephant' is written.

Before reading the story

● Have the children ever seen an elephant (in real-life or in a book or television programme)? What does an elephant look like? What colour is it? Show them some pictures of elephants (both realistic and stylised – not Elmer) and ask the children to describe them.

● Show the children the card bearing the word 'elephant', tracing it with a finger to emphasise the shapes of the letters, and, by using the words 'up' and 'down' pointing out the ascenders of the 'l', 'h' and 't', and the descender of the 'p'.

● Write or print, using a word processor, the words 'elephant', 'Elmer', 'yellow', 'red', 'orange', 'blue', 'green', 'purple', 'black' and 'white' on cards. Draw the shapes of the words on another set of cards, and ask the children to match the words to their shapes.

After reading the story

● Ask the children how all the animals in the jungle knew which elephant was Elmer, how Elmer was different from the other elephants, whether he liked being different at first and what made him want to change the way he looked. Can the children describe what Elmer did to change the way he looked, and why? Some of the children may be able to say what changed Elmer's mind, to make him enjoy being different.

● Ask the children to paint a picture of a real elephant. Using pictures of real elephants, draw attention to their shape, and special features such as their tusks and trunk. Help the children to mix grey paint using white and adding a little black.

● Provide elephant outlines (on A5 paper) on which the children can make up their own patterns using felt-tips. Their finished elephants can be used to form a border for a display (arrange them trunk-to-tail).

● Set up a 'writing' area in which the children can try to copy the word 'elephant' using a variety of media, such as felt-tips or pencils and paper, a tray of damp sand, and wooden or plastic letters.

The children tried to copy Elmer's patchwork pattern by gluing squares of coloured paper on to elephant outlines.

Assessment

● Can the children describe the shape and colour of a real elephant?

● Can they say how Elmer was different? Can they name the colours?

● How well do they mix grey from white and black paint?

● Can they make up colourful patterns with which to complete elephant outlines?

● Do they use a wide range of colours in their patterns?

● Can they sort a collection of coloured paper into separate colours, putting them into the correct boxes?

● Can they recognise and repeat sections of Elmer's pattern?

● Do the children recognise the word 'elephant'?

Evidence of the children's learning

The children looked at a picture of Elmer; some of them could name the shape of most his patches of colour. They looked for examples of squares from everyday life, such as biscuits, books, tiles, packets and greetings cards.

The children drew round plastic squares, then cut out square pieces of coloured paper, and glued them on to grey elephant shapes to make elephants which looked like Elmer. One or two of them wanted to copy Elmer's exact pattern from the book.

Differentiating the activities

To help children who have difficulty in recognising colours, remind them of Elmer's special pattern, showing them a picture of him. Talk about the colours of his skin. Give the children shoe boxes, each of which has been lined with a different colour, and ask them to cut small pieces from the coloured paper provided and to put them into the right boxes. The number of colours could be limited according to the ability of the children.

Extension activities

Show the children a copy of the book and talk about the pattern of colours on Elmer's skin. Provide tracings of Elmer (from the cover of the book) and ask the children to colour their 'Elmer' tracings so that they look the same as him. This might be easier if just one row at a time is uncovered. They could cut out their elephant, draw around it on grey paper, and then cut out this new elephant outline. Attach the grey elephant in the form of a flap to cover the patterned one.

The children can use their paper Elmer when they take turns to retell parts of the story, keeping the grey flap down during the parts when Elmer is grey and lifting it during the parts where he is multi-coloured.

Involving parents

Encourage parents to find other multi-coloured patterns (for example on wallpaper, fabrics, wrapping paper, and greetings cards) and to talk to the children about them, using the word 'multi-coloured'. They could talk to the children about the colours, pointing out and naming some of them.

Parents could help to dress the children in multi-coloured outfits so that they can have an 'Elmer day' like that described in the book.

Other books to use

The Mixed-Up Chameleon
by Eric Carle (Picture Puffins)

The chameleon spends its time catching flies, and changing colour. It is happy and contented until it visits the zoo and sees the animals there. Then it wants not only to change colour but to change shape – to be like the exciting animals it sees. It wishes it could be big and white like a polar bear, then handsome like a flamingo, then smart like a fox and so on. The illustrations show the ways in which the chameleon changes as each of its wishes comes true. The chameleon is not happy with any of the changes; in the end, it wishes he could be itself. Once again the wish comes true – and it catches a fly.

Ask the children to look at each picture of the chameleon in turn, describing how it has changed from the last one; at first only its colour changes – until it starts wishing to be like other animals. The children should notice the ways in which the chameleon's colour matches its surroundings. They could copy a picture of the chameleon, still looking like itself, matching the colours they use to those on the picture in the book. They could a paint a separate picture of the background on which the chameleon is seen, then cut out their picture of the chameleon and glue it onto the background. Can they see it from a distance?

Point out the textures of the coloured parts of the chameleon in the picture showing the chameleon looking 'funny like a seal', by which time it is made up of bits of many animals. The children could make coloured, textured paper by making rubbings by rubbing wax crayons over textured white wallpaper, put feathers and other flat textured objects underneath paper of different colours and make wax crayon rubbings.

With the children, make a big book which tells the story of the chameleon's changes. The children could use felt-tips to colour their pictures to look like those in the book. Cut the pages like those in the book so that the reader can easily find the page by looking at the notches. Write some of the words from the story below the pictures. Some of the children might be able to help with this.

My Presents
by Rod Campbell (Campbell Books)

The children lift the flaps in this book to find out what is the birthday present inside each parcel. The descriptions help them to guess what is under the flap, but so too does the shape of the parcel.

Talk about the shapes of the parcels, and what they have been wrapped in: a bag, paper, or a box. Ask the children to describe the colour and pattern of each one: it might have stripes, wavy lines or spots, for example. Which do they like best and why?

Show them a collection of materials for wrapping presents and ask them to choose one to copy. See if they can find repeating patterns on the paper. The children could use felt-tips or crayons to make their own wrapping-paper pattern; or they could print a repeating pattern using a range of materials for printing, such as kitchen utensils (for example pastry-cutters and biscuit-cutters).

Sounds and music

Responding to:
Peace at Last
by Jill Murphy (Picture Puffins)

Intended learning

For the children to learn about the ways in which sounds can be described in stories, to listen to and to re-create sounds using their voices. To develop the children's ability to find out, by using pictures in a book, what is happening in the story.

The story

The story is about a sleepless night: Mr and Mrs Bear and Baby Bear are tired, so they go to bed; Mrs Bear falls asleep but Mr Bear doesn't. Mrs Bear starts to snore, so Mr Bear has to find some peace and quiet. He goes into Baby Bear's room. Not only is Baby Bear awake, but he is pretending to be an aeroplane, complete with sound effects!

Mr Bear tries to find a peaceful place to sleep in other places around the house and garden, but to no avail; eventually he tries the car. Just as he is dropping off to sleep the birds start to sing and the sun begins to shine. He gives up and goes back into the house where Mrs Bear has stopped snoring and Baby Bear is sleeping peacefully. "Peace at last," says Mr Bear to himself – just before the alarm clock goes off!

Key vocabulary

aeroplane, alarm-clock, cat, clock, cuckoo, drip, hedgehog, miaow, owl, sing, snore, snuffle, tick-tock, too-whit-too-whoo, tweet

The activity

You will need:

a tape-recording of 'night-time' and 'morning' sounds, pictures of the things which make these sounds, a cassette player, pictures of the things which make the sounds in the story cards on which their sounds have been written, two spare copies of the book, scissors, glue, paper, mail order catalogues, magazines and brochures;

spare copies of the book from which pictures of the things which make the sounds have been cut out, glued onto A5 cards and laminated, separate cards on which are written the words for each sound which kept Mr Bear awake; snore, nyaaow (aeroplane noise made by Baby Bear), tick-tock, cuckoo, drip drip, hmmmmm-mmmmm, too-whit-too-whoo, snuffle, miaaaow, tweet tweet, and brrrrrrrrrr;

a role-play corner to represent the Bear family's home, including all the things which make the sounds (real, models or pictures) and three teddy bears; mail order catalogues, brochures, scissors, glue, paper.

Before reading the story

● Ask the children what they do after they have been put to bed at night. Do they go straight to sleep or do they play? What do they play? Do their parents know when they are not asleep? What do they do?

● Ask the children what they do when they hear their parents coming to check whether or not they are asleep. Ask them about the things which keep them awake at night. What do they do to try to get to sleep? Record their responses.

After reading the story

● The children could listen to a tape recording of 'morning sounds' and 'night-time sounds' and match them to pictures of the things which make them. They could put the pictures in the order in which their sounds are heard on the tape.

● Ask the children to match pictures from spare copies of the book to cards on which their sounds are written. An adult could help them to read the sounds.

● Small groups of children could take turns to act the story in a role-play corner; ask them to include all the sounds in the story. They could add some sounds of their own.

● Ask a group of children to cut out pictures of things which make sounds and glue them onto a sheet of paper. During 'discussion time' they could demonstrate the sounds to the rest of the class, asking the other children to identify them.

● Make a classroom display entitled 'Peace at Last', which shows the children's paintings of the things which kept Mr Bear awake. Add some of the words of the story, including those which describe the sounds.

We set up a sound table and the children talked about the different sounds they could make.

Assessment

● Can the children talk about the sounds they hear when they are in bed?

● Can they make these sounds using their voices?

● Can they 'fill in the gaps' when the story is re-read with the sounds omitted?

● When listening to tape recordings, can the children match sounds to the objects which make them?

● Can they join in role-play of the story using appropriate sounds?

● Are the children able to sort sounds into 'long' and 'short'?

● Can they match some of the words for sounds to the pictures in the book which show when they happen?

Evidence of the children's learning

We talked about the sounds which kept Mr Bear awake, and re-read the story, omitting the words which describe the sounds, inviting the children to 'fill in the gaps'. The children took turns to retell parts of the story, replacing each sound with one which Mr Bear might have heard in their own homes, for example: traffic going past, a chiming clock, a car alarm, a burglar alarm, people calling to one another or singing, a dog barking or a baby crying. They used their voices to make each sound.

We set up a 'sounds' table in the classroom which included a range of objects which the children could use to experiment with sound effects.

Differentiating the activities

Help the children to make the sounds from the story. They could take turns to make a sound while the others have to guess what it is. With help, they could change the sounds in the story so that different things kept Mr Bear awake: for example, a noisy car, the wind howling, the branches of a tree tapping against the window, a thunderstorm, hailstones hitting the roof and trains rumbling along a nearby railway.

Extension activities

The children could make up their own stories in which they try to sleep but something keeps them awake. What do they do about it? Do they try to sleep in a different place, or cover their heads, as Mr Bear did? Where do they finally fall asleep? But what wakes them? Encourage them to use their voices to make the sounds. An adult could transcribe the words for the sounds for the children to copy or trace.

Some of the children might be able to identify different kinds of sounds: short sounds like the tick-tock of the clock, and longer sounds like Mrs Bear's snoring. They could identify similar kinds of sounds in and around the school.

Ask them to listen for sounds which repeat, like the ticking of a clock or the ringing of a telephone.

Involving parents

Parents could sit in silence with their child, listening. They could talk about the sounds they hear, saying what is making them. This should be a short session of a minute or two. Provide notebooks in which parents can record what they and the children have heard. They could try listening for 'morning sounds', 'night-time sounds', 'Saturday sounds', 'swimming pool sounds, 'park sounds' and 'shop sounds'.

Other books to use

Goodnight Owl
by Pat Hutchins (Picture Puffins)

Owl is trying to sleep, but it's day-time and the other animals are making a lot of noise: the bees buzz, the squirrel cracks nuts, the crows croak, the woodpecker pecks, the starlings chitter, the jays scream, and so on. All this noise keeps Owl awake. As night falls the animals become tired; soon they are all fast asleep – then Owl screeches and wakes them all up!

Talk about the different sounds made by the animals: read the words which describe the sounds and then the words for the sounds themselves, and ask the children to use their voices to make the sounds, for example: the bees buzzed ('buzz, buzz'); the crows croaked ('caw, caw'), the starlings chittered ('twit-twit, twit-twit'), and so on. Then read the story, reading only the words which describe the sound (buzzed, croaked, chittered, and so on), and ask the children to make the sounds.

The children could make up their own stories replacing the animals with others they know, such as cats, mice, a snake and a donkey (which could be under the tree).

Noisy Farm
by Rod Campbell (Picture Puffins)

The farm wakes up to the sound of the rooster as it crows and there are many more noises to be heard as the reader follows Sam the dog on his journey of discovery around the farm. Each double-page ends with a question about a sound, whose source is discovered when the page is turned.

If possible, play a tape-recording of the animals in the story and invite the children to copy the sounds using their voices. They could choose an animal and copy the sound it makes at appropriate points while the story is being read.

The Train Ride
by June Crebbin (Walker Books)

The story describes all the things a little girl sees through the windows of a train as she goes with her mother to visit her grandma. It is written in the rhythm of a train.

Read the story, ensuring that the train rhythm is clear to the children. Re-read it, inviting them to join in. Talk about other things which might be seen from train windows (if possible, take the children on a short train journey and talk about some of the things which they see through the windows), and about what these things look like or what they are doing.

The children could take turns to retell parts of the story, substituting things they saw from their train journey (or which they think might be seen), for example: 'Houses for people, Who are out at work', 'Children playing, Laughing and shouting', and 'Dogs on leads, And cats in trees'. Help them to practise their own parts of the story, repeating them with a 'train' rhythm. Groups of children could perform the story which they have practised.

Books featured in Responding to Stories

Personal and Social Development

Avocado Baby by John Burningham (Red Fox)
A Birthday Cake for Little Bear by Max Welthuijs (North South Books)
The Blanket by John Burningham (Red Fox)
Bread and Jam for Frances by Russell and Lillian Hoban (Picture Puffins)
Cleversticks by Bernard Ashley (Collins Picture Lions)
Handa's Surprise by Eileen Browne (Walker)
Happy Birthday Sam by Pat Hutchins (Picture Puffins)
Heaven by Nicholas Allan (Hutchinson)
Jack's Tummy by Katharine McEwen (Chart Books)
Kim's Magic Tree by Verna Allette Wilkins (Tamarind)
The Magical Bicycle by Berlie Doherty and Christian Birmingham (Collins Picture Lions)
My Presents by Rod Campbell (Campbell Books)
Noisy Farm by Rod Campbell (Picture Puffins)
This is Our House by Michael Rosen (Walker)
The Tiny Seed by Eric Carle (Puffin)
What Makes Me Happy? by Catherine and Laurence Anholt (Walker)
What's that Noise? by Francesca Simon and David Melby (Hodder)
Who Can Tell? by Stuart Henson (Hutchinson)
Why is the Sky Blue? by Sally Grindley and Susan Varley (Andersen Press)

Language and Literature

Buster's Day by Rod Campbell (Campbell Books)
Don't Forget the Bacon by Pat Hutchins (Picture Puffins)
Do You Want to be My Friend? by Eric Carle (Picture Puffins)
My Presents by Rod Campbell (Campbell Books)
Noisy Farm by Rod Campbell (Picture Puffins)
This is the Bear by Sarah Hughes and Helen Craig (Walker)
We're Going on a Bear Hunt by Michael Rosen (Walker)

Mathematics

The Bad Tempered Ladybird by Eric Carle (Picture Puffins)
Henry's Ball by Rod Campbell (Campbell Books)
Mum Can Fix It Verna Allette Wilkins (Tamarind)
One Bear at Bedtime by Mick Inkpen (Hodder)
Rooster's Off to See the World by Eric Carle (Puffin)

Rosie's Walk by Pat Hutchins (Picture Puffins)
Ten Little Crocodiles by Colin West (Walker)
Time For Bed by Alexis Obi (Tamarind)
Time to Get Up by Gill McLean (Tamarind)
The Very Hungry Caterpillar by Eric Carle (Picture Puffins)

Knowledge and Understanding of the World

The Baby by John Burningham (Red Fox)
Cat Among the Cabbages by Alison Bartlett (Levinson Books)
Each Peach Pear Plum by Janet & Allan Ahlberg (Picture Puffins)
From Snowflakes to Sandcastles by Annie Owen (Frances Lincoln)
Jack and the Beanstalk Traditional (Ladybird Books)
Mr Wolf's Week by Colin Hawkins (Mammoth)
Once there were Giants by Martin Waddell (Walker)
The Train Ride by June Crebbin (Walker)
The Very Hungry Caterpillar by Eric Carle (Picture Puffins)
Who Sank the Boat? by Pamela Allen (Picture Puffins)

Physical Development

Buster's Day by Rod Campbell (Campbell Books)
Cat Among the Cabbages by Alison Bartlett (Levinson Books)
I'm Going on a Dragon Hunt by Maurice Jones (Puffin)
Little Bird by Rod Campbell (Campbell Books)
We're Going on a Bear Hunt by Michael Rosen (Walker)

Creative Development

Elmer by David McKee (Red Fox)
Goodnight Owl by Pat Hutchins (Picture Puffins)
The Mixed-up Chameleon by Eric Carle (Picture Puffins)
My Presents by Rod Campbell (Campbell Books)
Noisy Farm by Rod Campbell (Picture Puffins)
Peace at Last by Jill Murphy (Picture Puffins)
The Train Ride by June Crebbin (Walker)

First published 1998 by A & C Black (Publishers) Ltd 35 Bedford Row, London WC1R 4JH
Text copyright © 1998 Christine Moorcroft. Illustrations © 1998 Alison Dexter.
All photographs by Zul Mukhida except: pp 29, 33, 45; David Spinner. Cover photograph by Alex Brattell.
The author and publisher would like to thank the staff and children of Sand Dunes Nursery, Seaforth and Greenacre Nursery, Bootle, Jane Salazar and Charlotte, Daniel, Emma and their mothers for their generous help in the preparation of this book.

ISBN 0-7136-4855-4
A CIP catalogue record for this book is available from the British Library.

Printed in China through Colorcraft Ltd.